WATCH OUT FOR THE PIKA

Drawings by
Betsy Streeter

ISBN: 978-0-9777264-7-9

First Printed: May 2020

Hello and thank you for visiting this collection of spontaneous drawings, paper and graphite and eraser bits that have become friends. Many of them contain bad animal puns, such as Duck in Chucks or Toucan in Vans (there are actually two spats puns in here, see if you can find them both). There are tardigrade puns too, like Bardigrade (I knew him, Horatio) and Yardigrade. I am aware how dreadful these are.

These drawings are a bit of a peek into my day to day life, in which I generally wake up with my head filled with ideas and throughout the day get them onto an available piece of paper.

Many of these fellows came into being during the COVID-19 lockdown of 2020 in California, during which I spent a great deal of time drawing, which is what I was doing before that and which I will most likely be doing afterward.

In fact, I'd like to dedicate this book to the friends and families of all types and configurations who have been doing that hard and lonely work of looking out for each other from afar, checking in through phones and screens and windows, asking after one another, helping blunt the force of the terrible waves of fear and uncertainty that this experience has brought.

I hope that this time gives way to a period when we can mend our ways, show that we care, and feel proud when we are generous with each other.

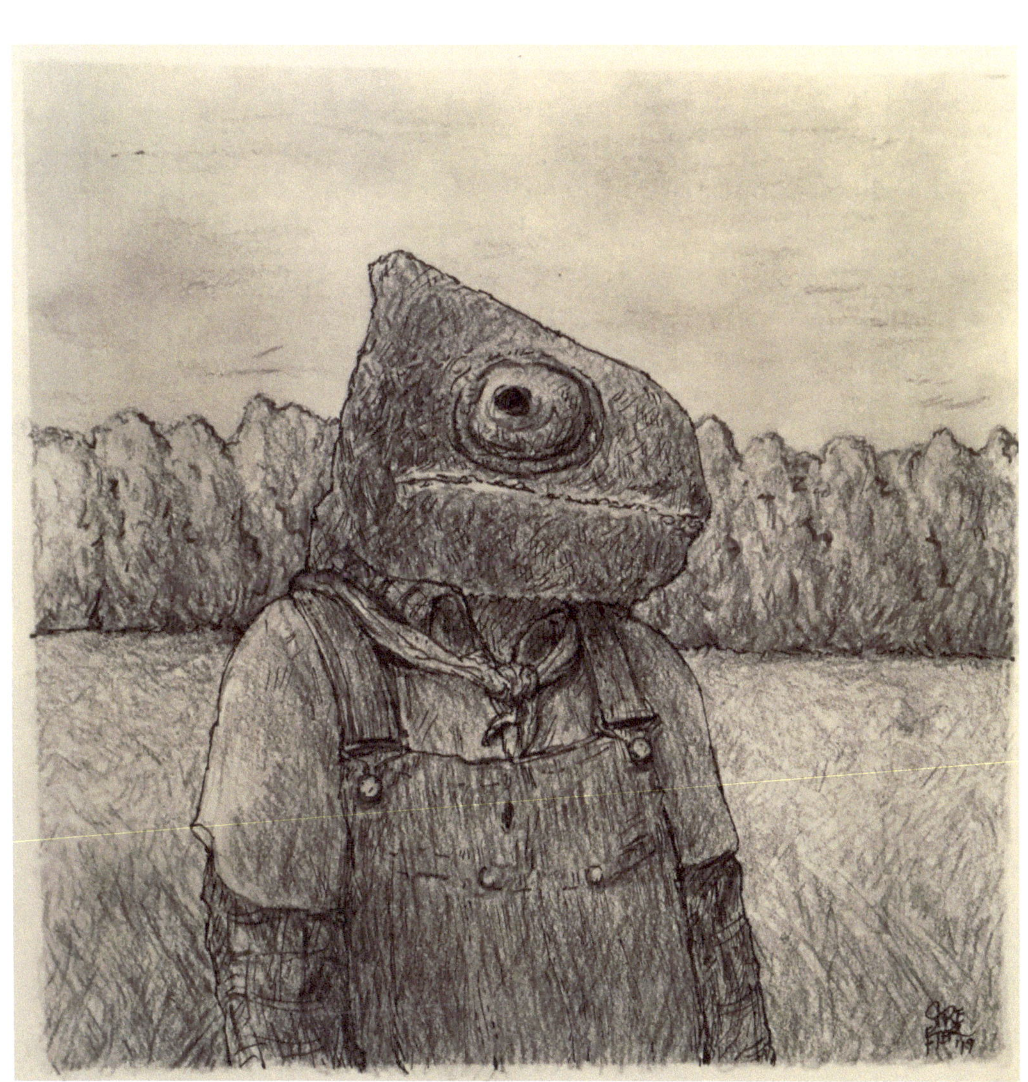

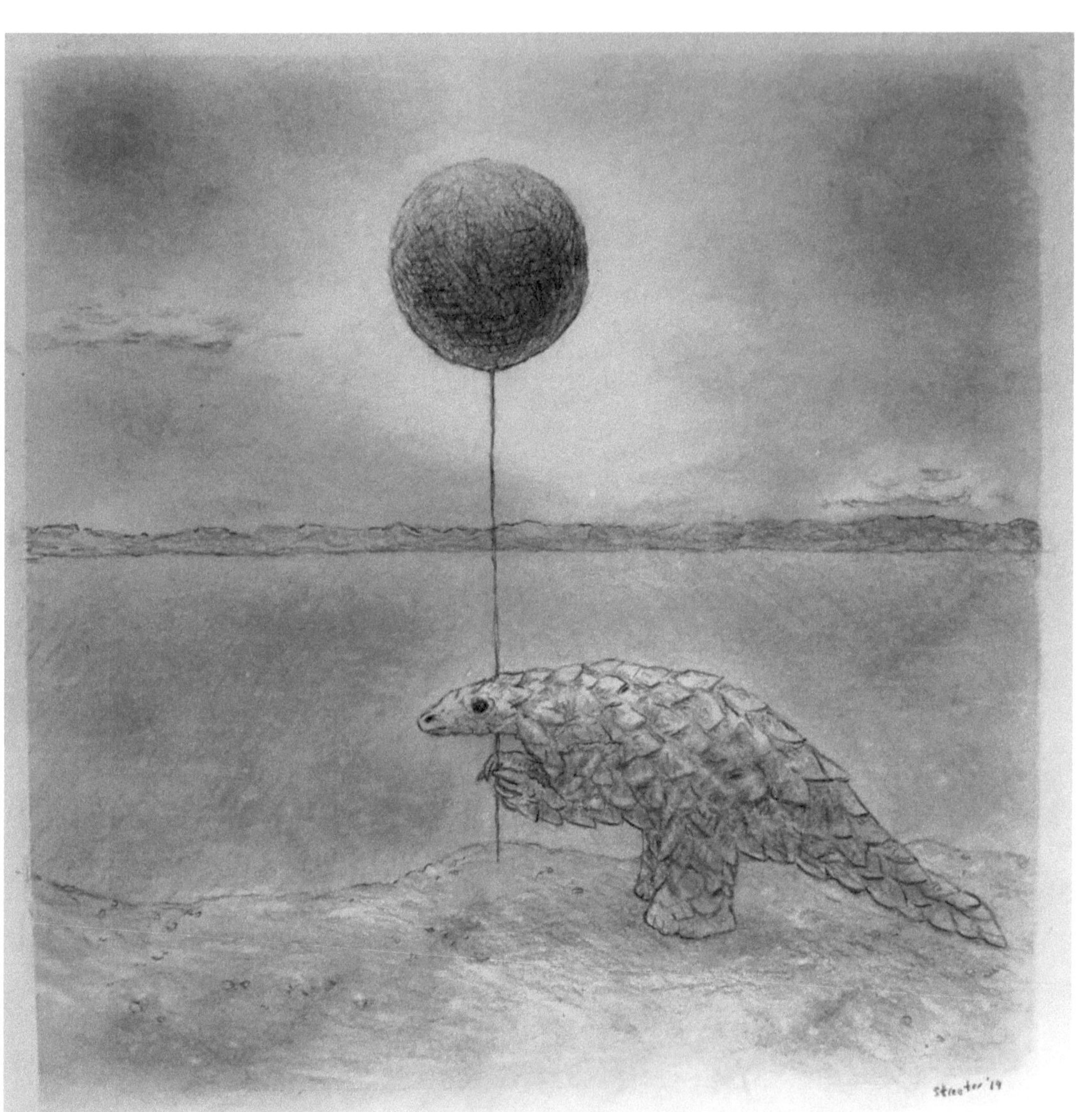

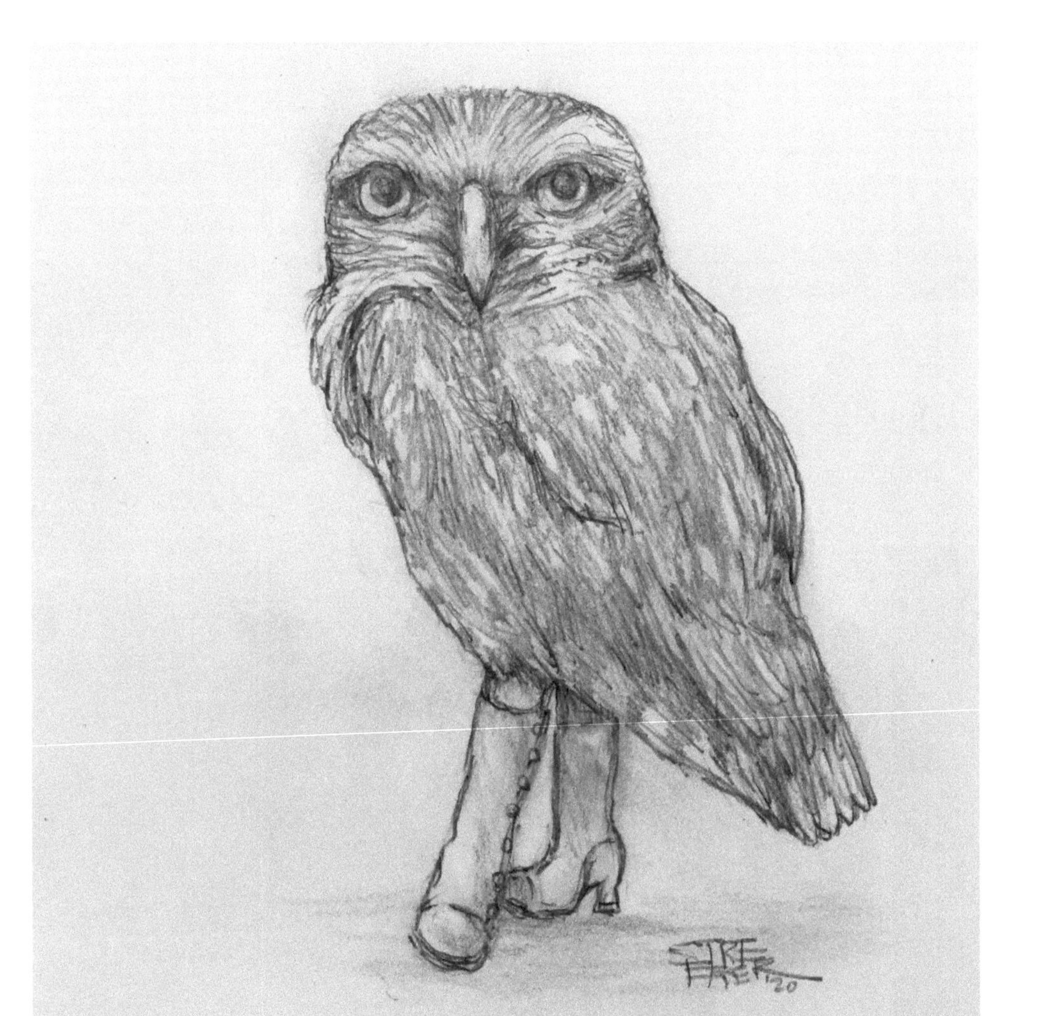

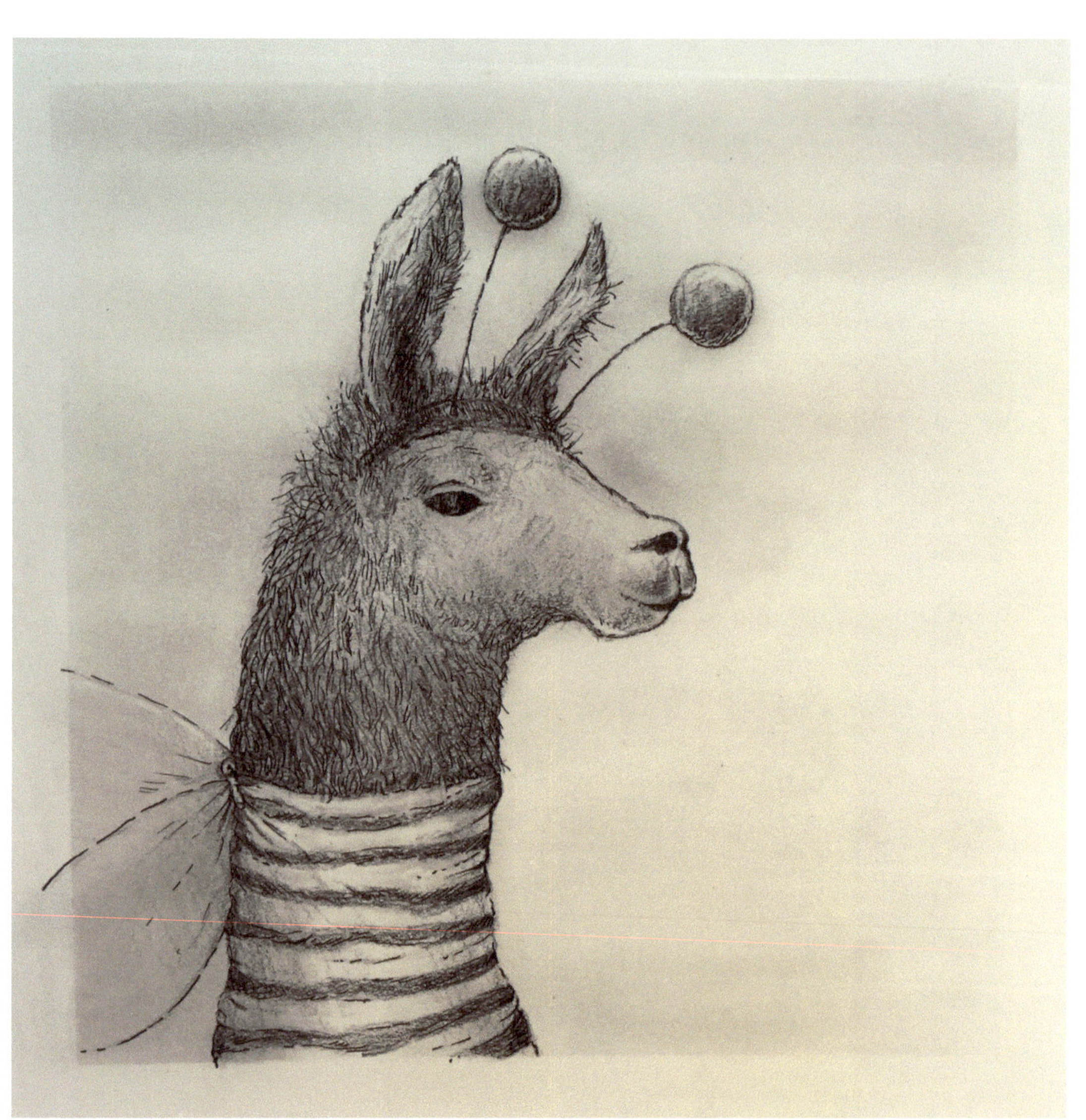

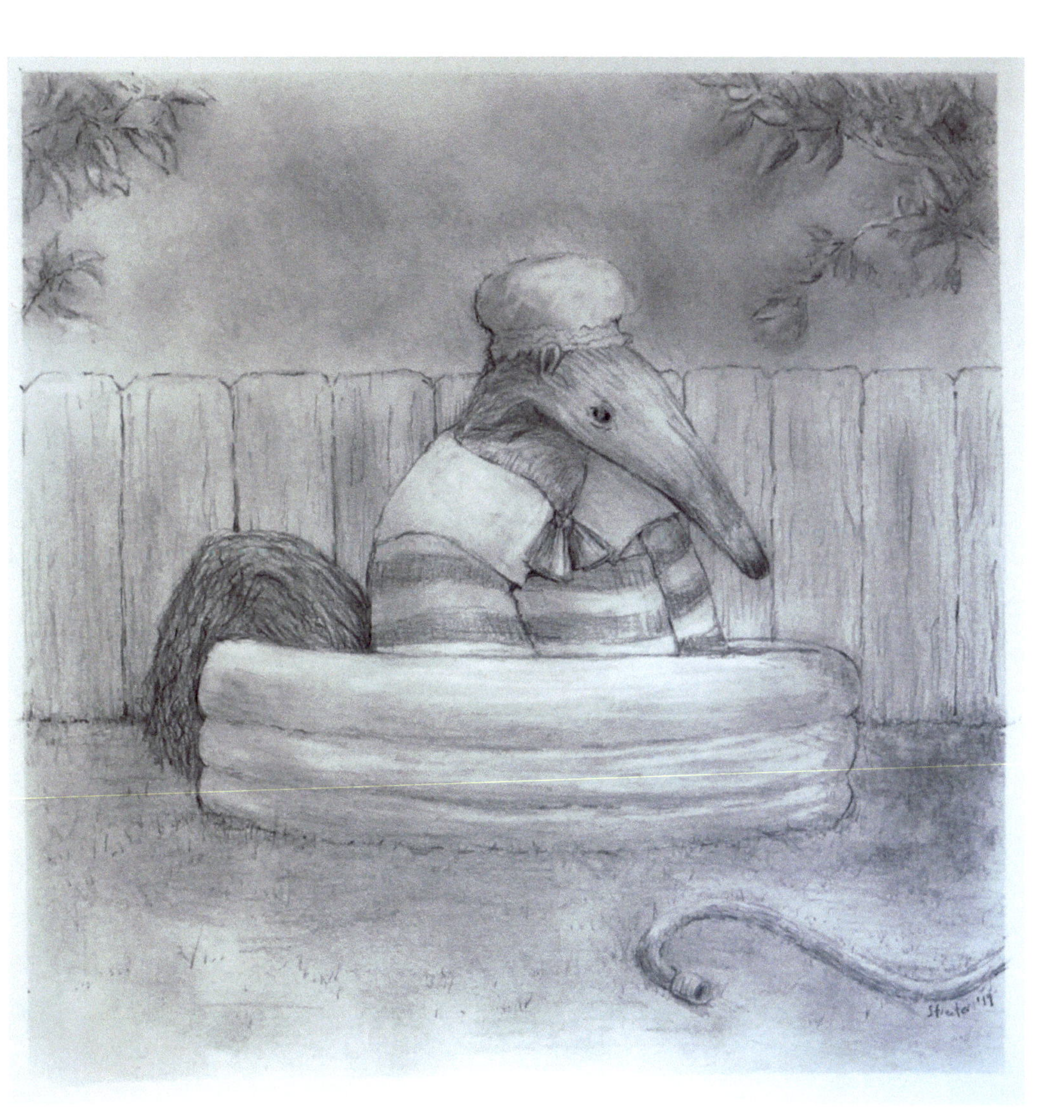

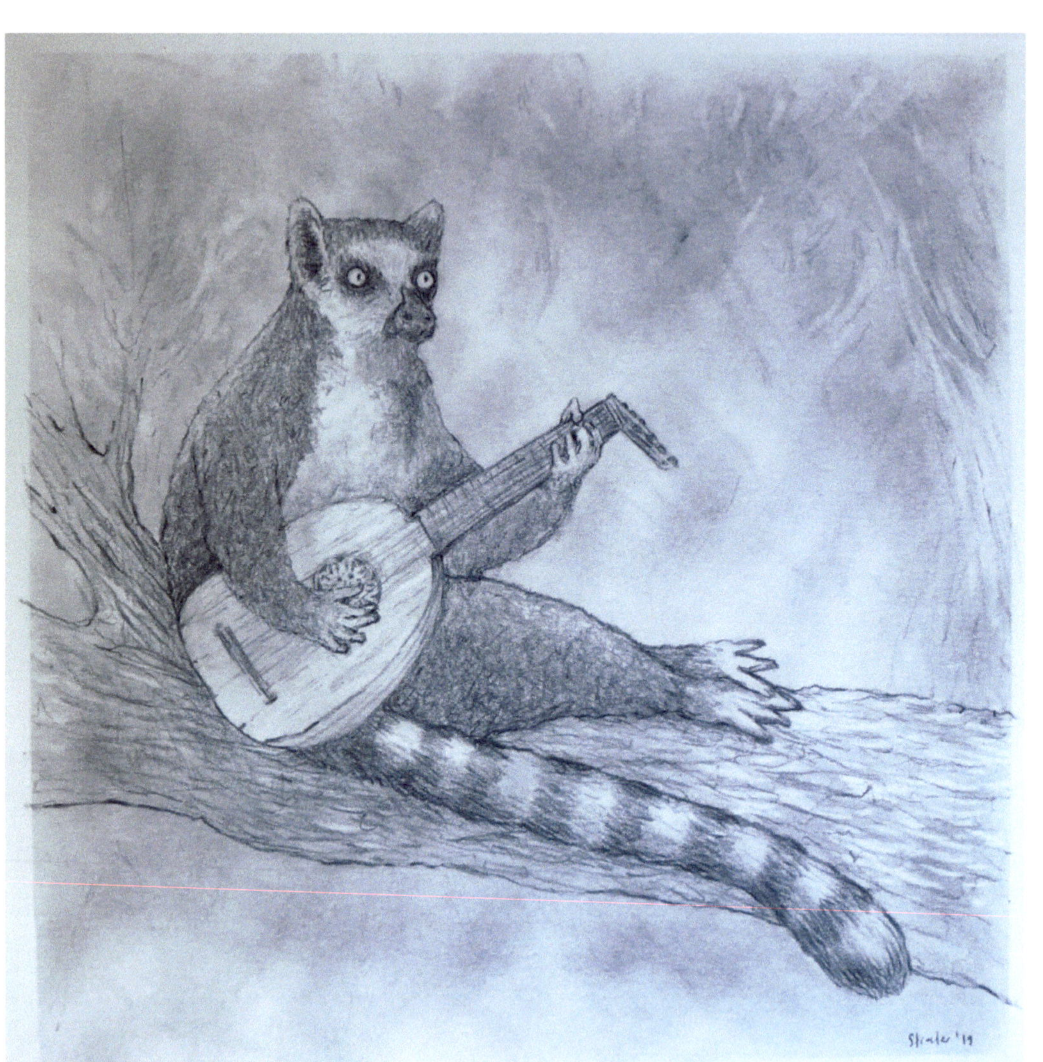

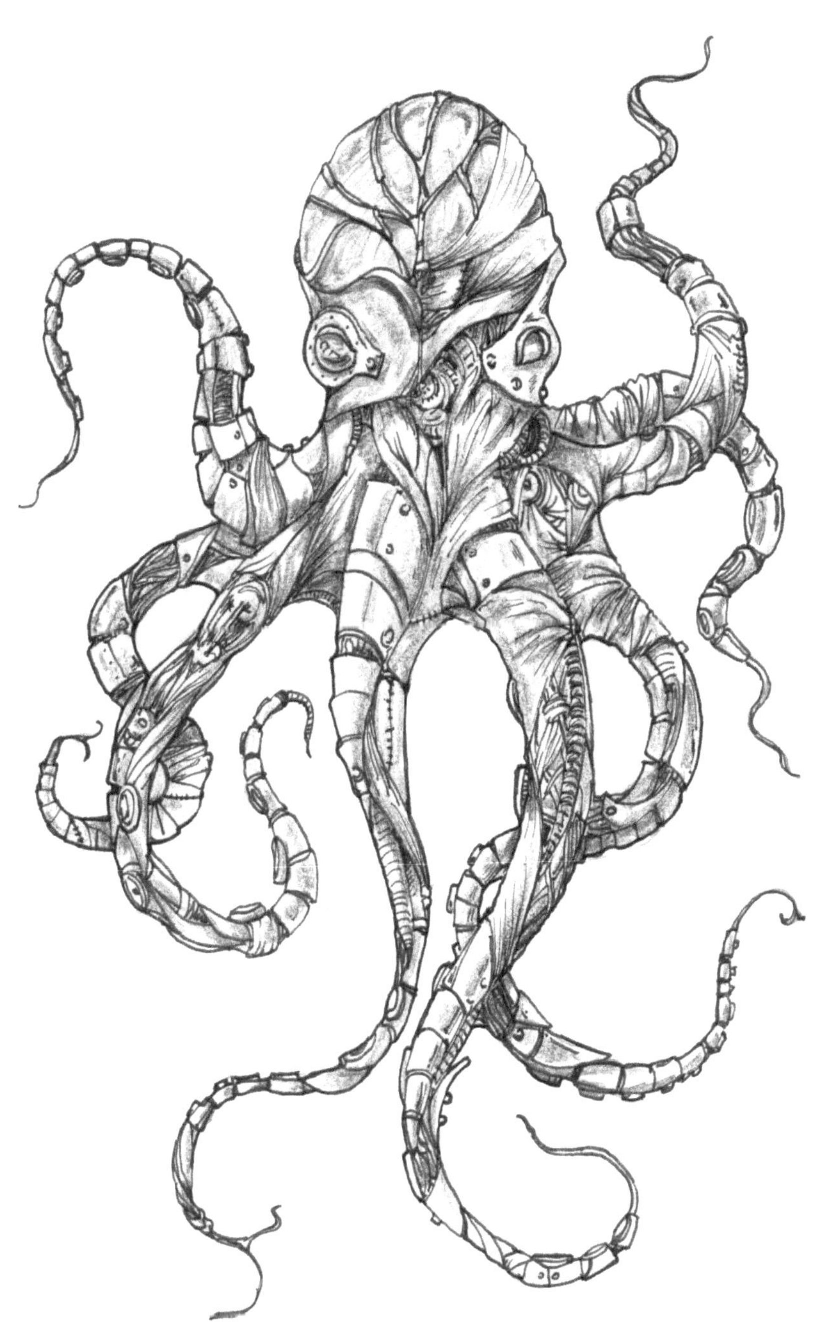

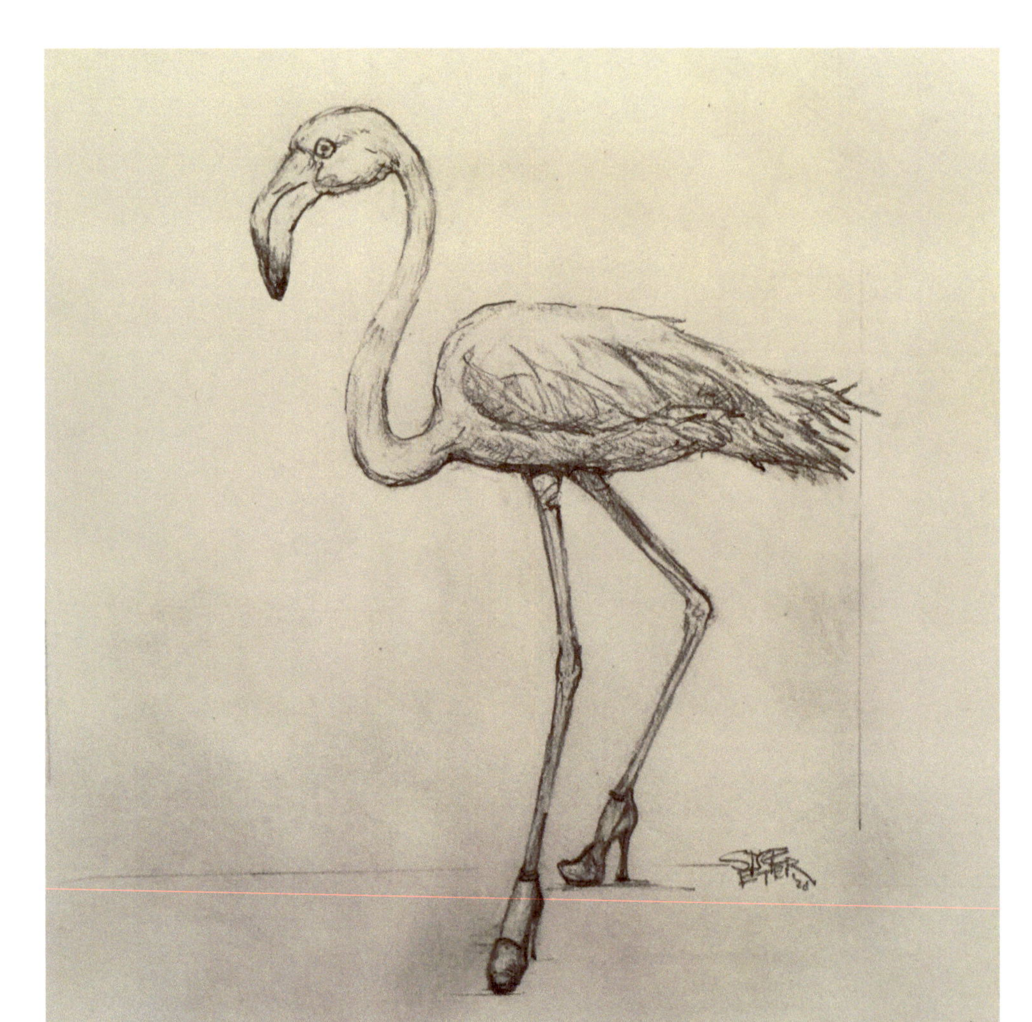

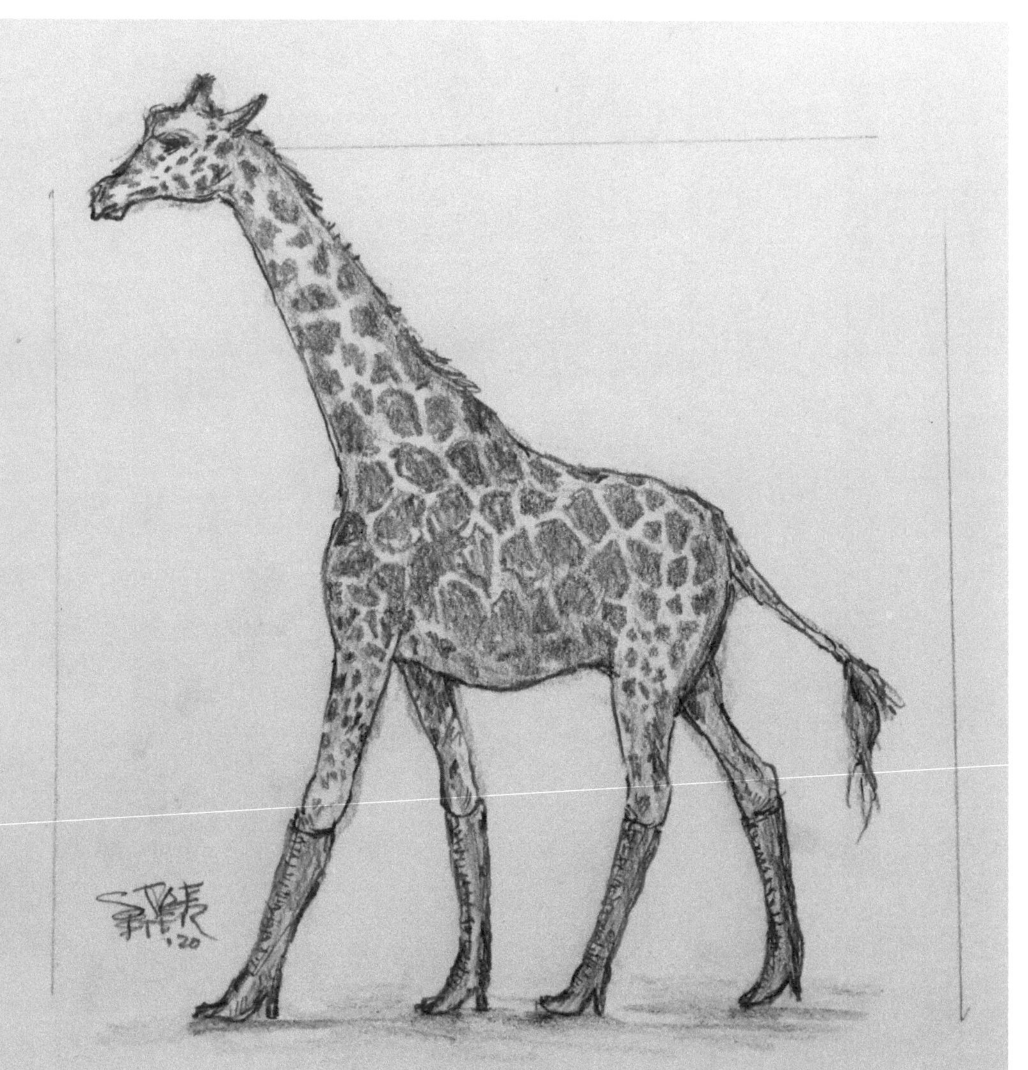

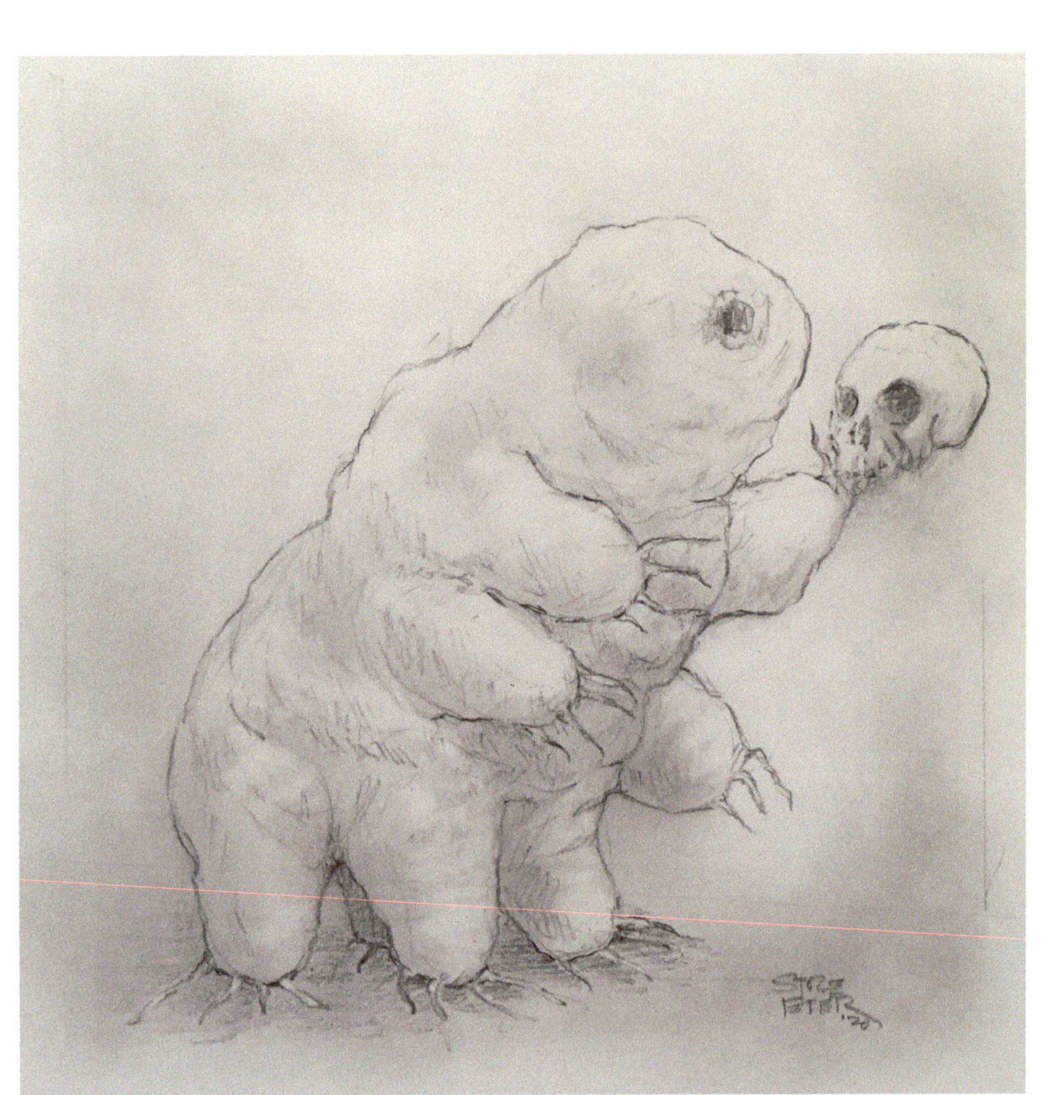

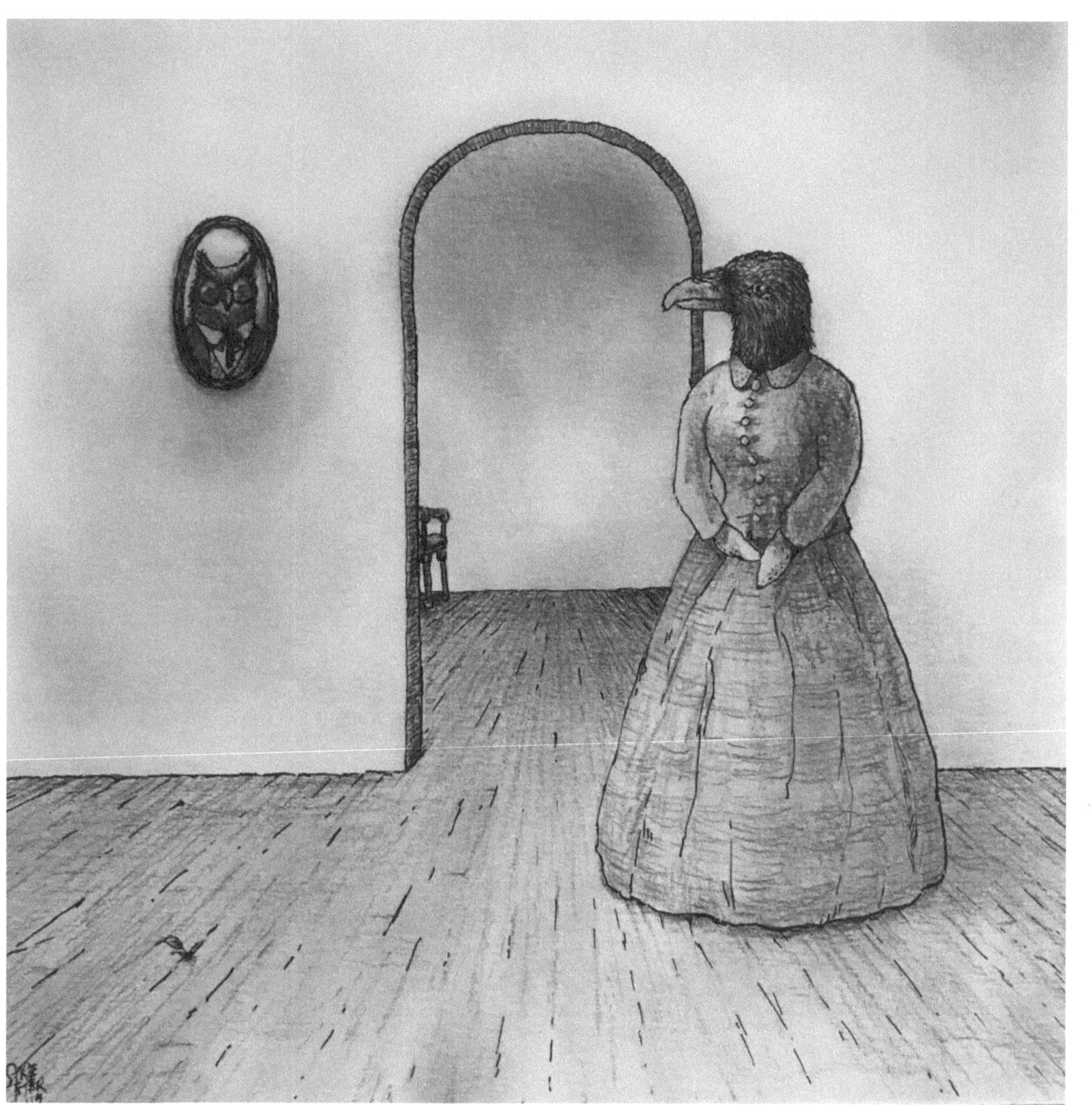

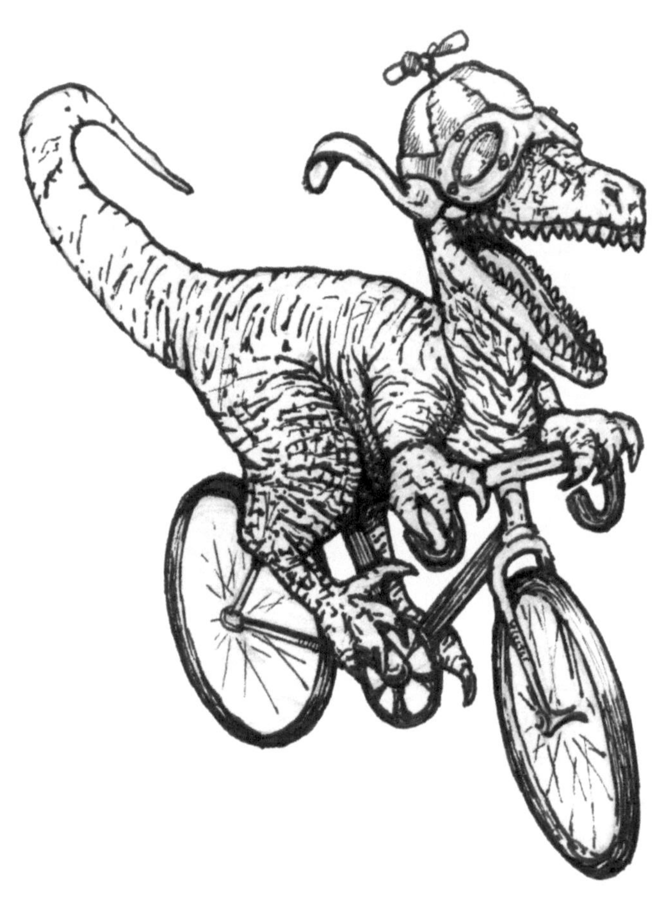

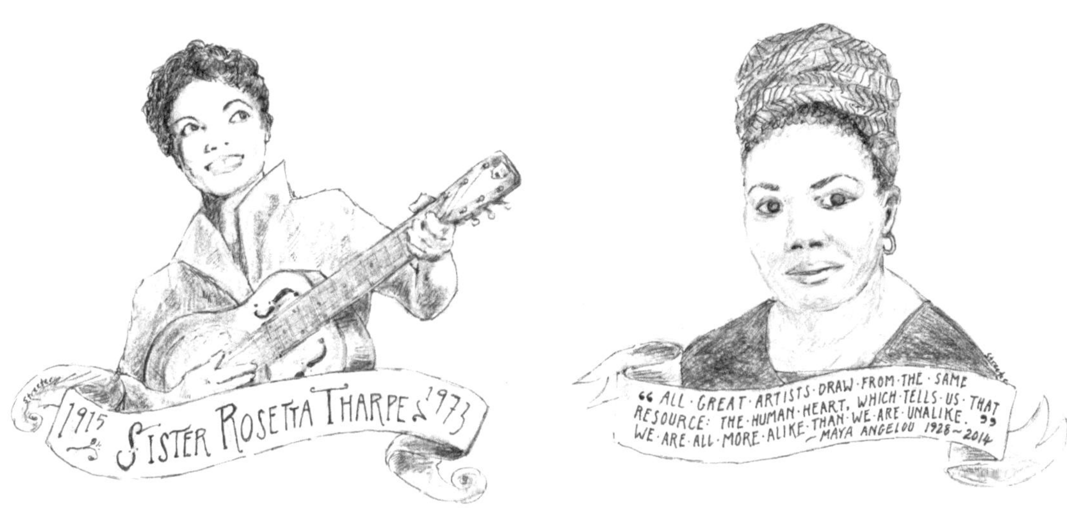

1915 · SISTER ROSETTA THARPE · 1973
" ALL · GREAT · ARTISTS · DRAW · FROM · THE · SAME
RESOURCE: THE · HUMAN · HEART, WHICH · TELLS · US · THAT
WE · ARE · ALL · MORE · ALIKE · THAN · WE · ARE · UNALIKE. "
— MAYA ANGELOU 1928 ~ 2014

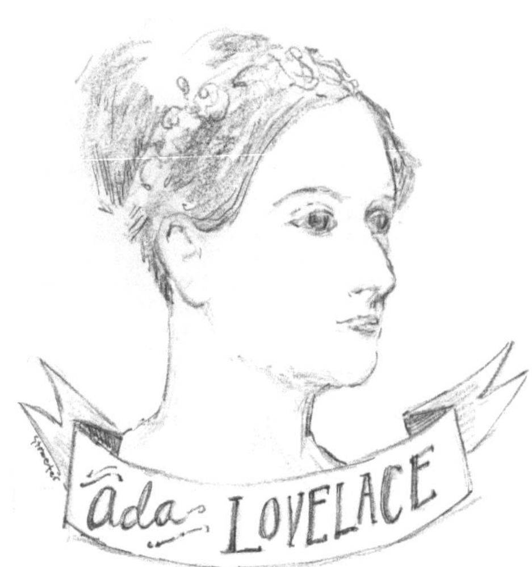

ada LOVELACE

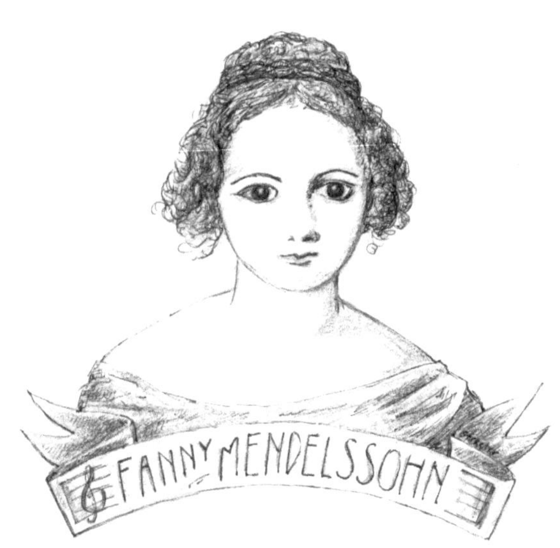

FANNY MENDELSSOHN

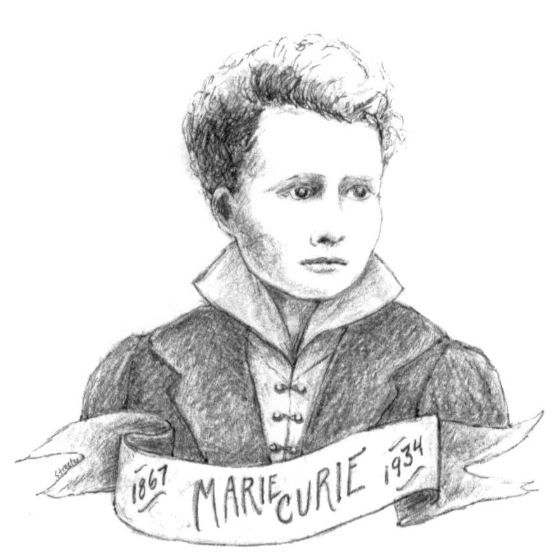

1867
MARIE CURIE
1934

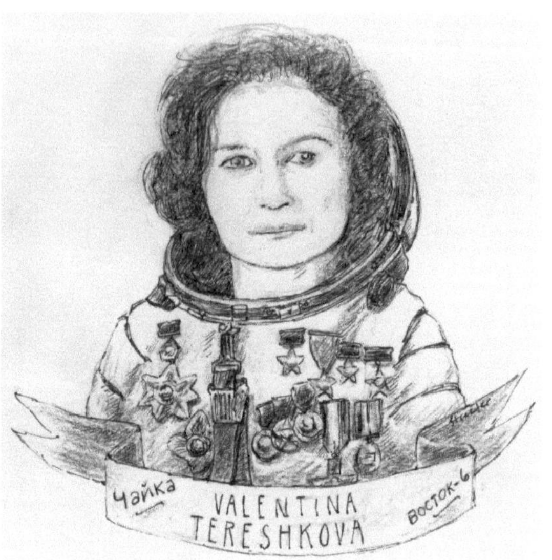

Чайка
VALENTINA
TERESHKOVA
ВОСТОК-6

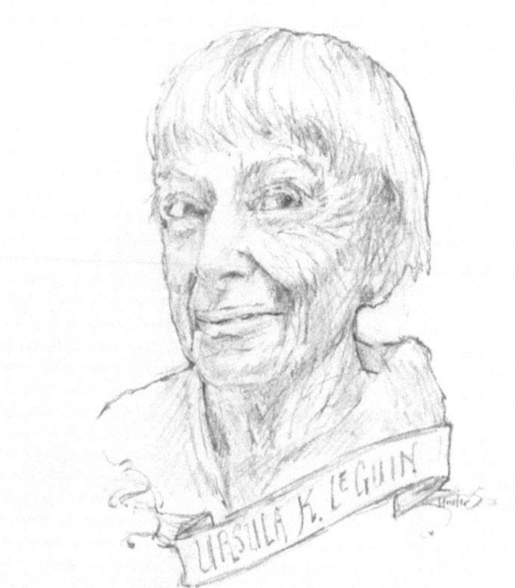

URSULA K. LE GUIN

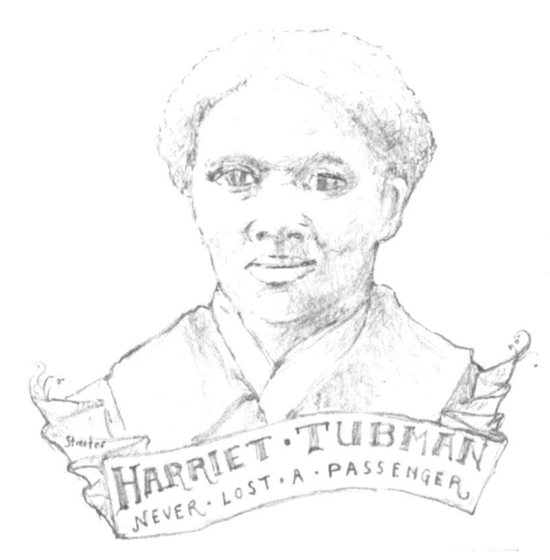

HARRIET · TUBMAN
NEVER · LOST · A · PASSENGER

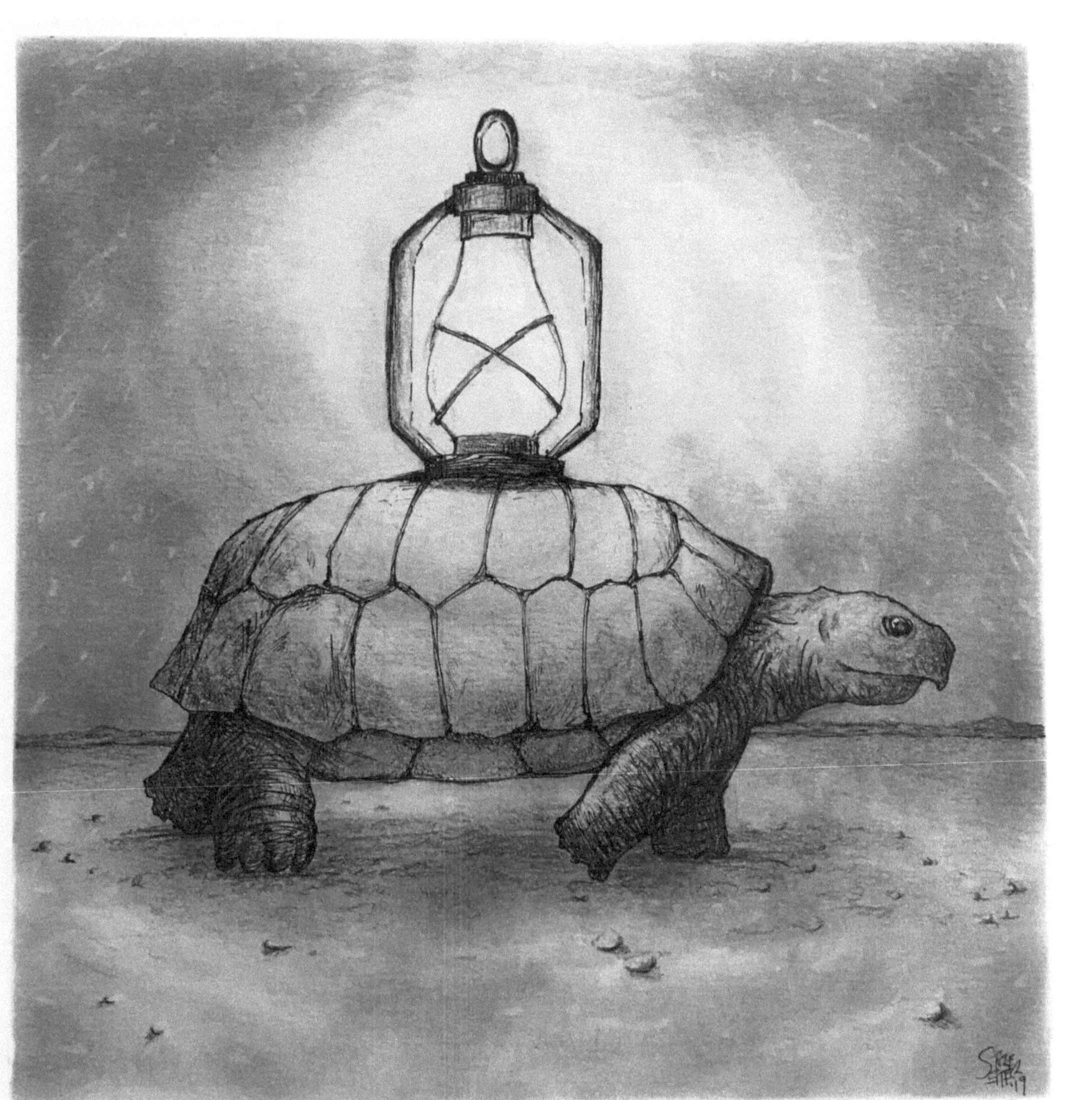

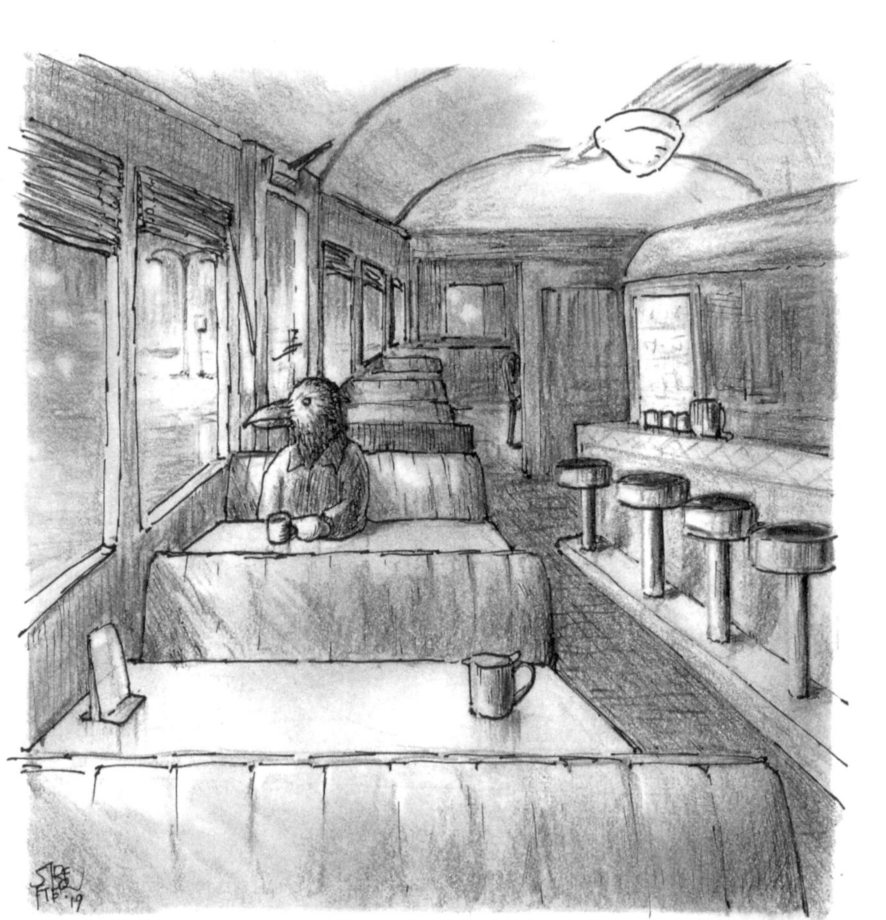

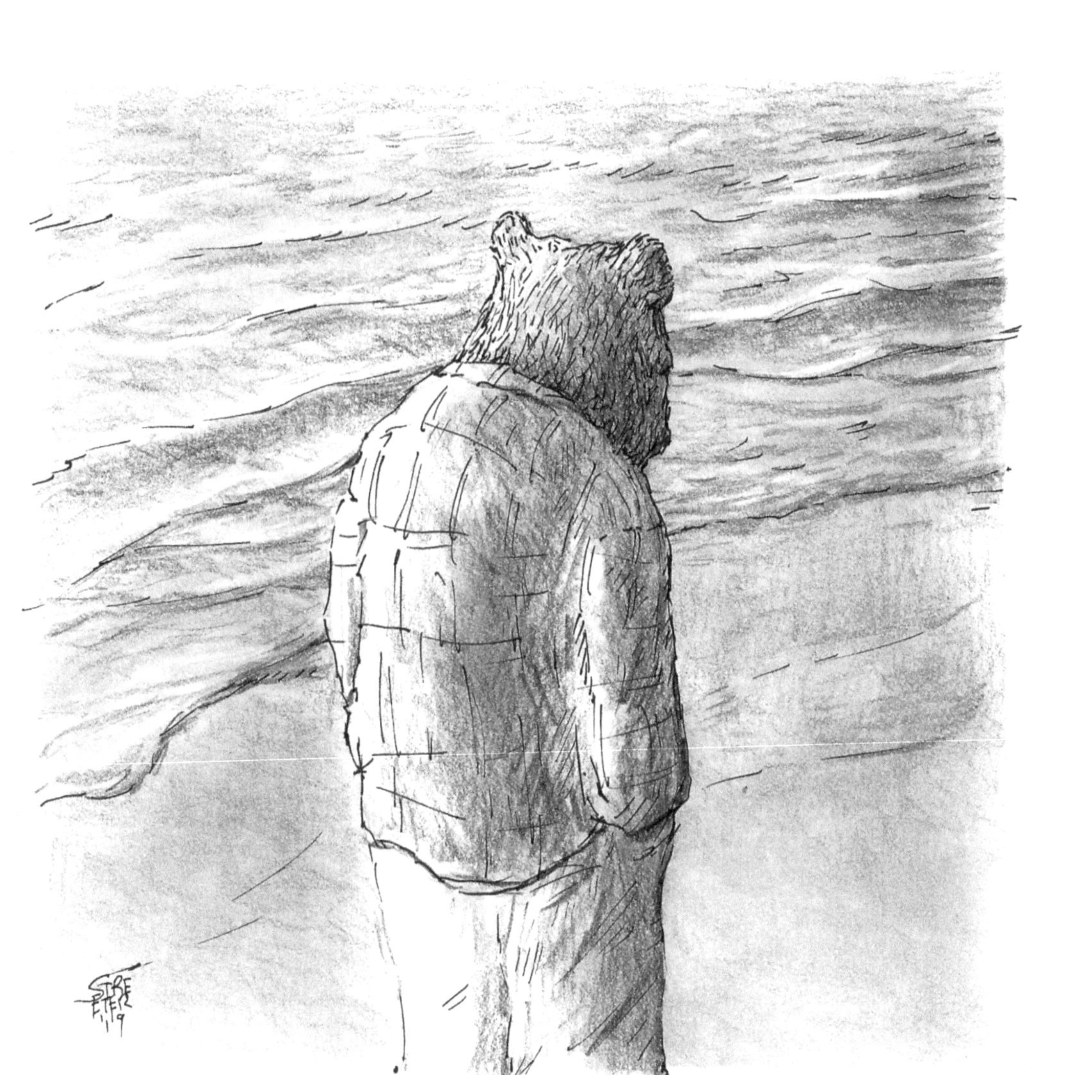

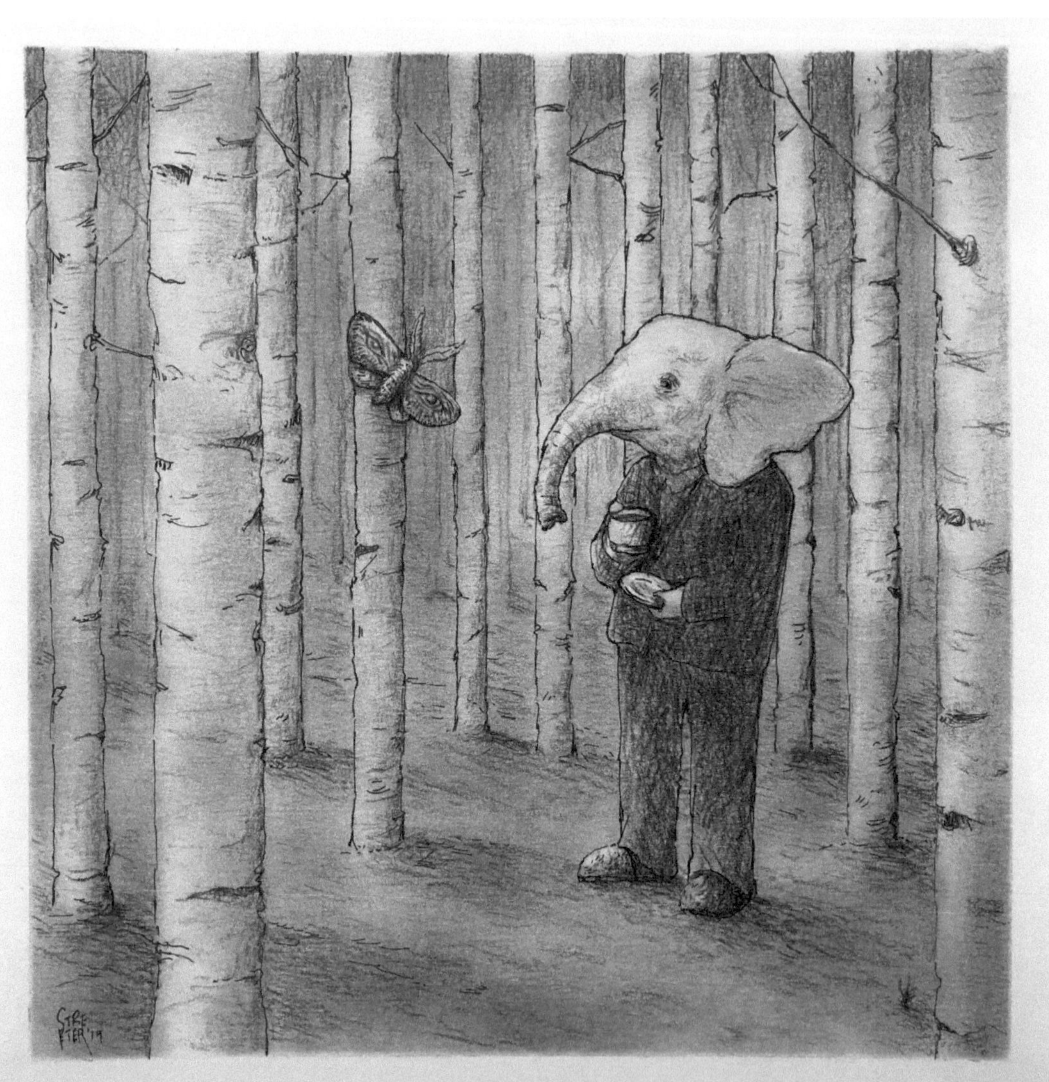

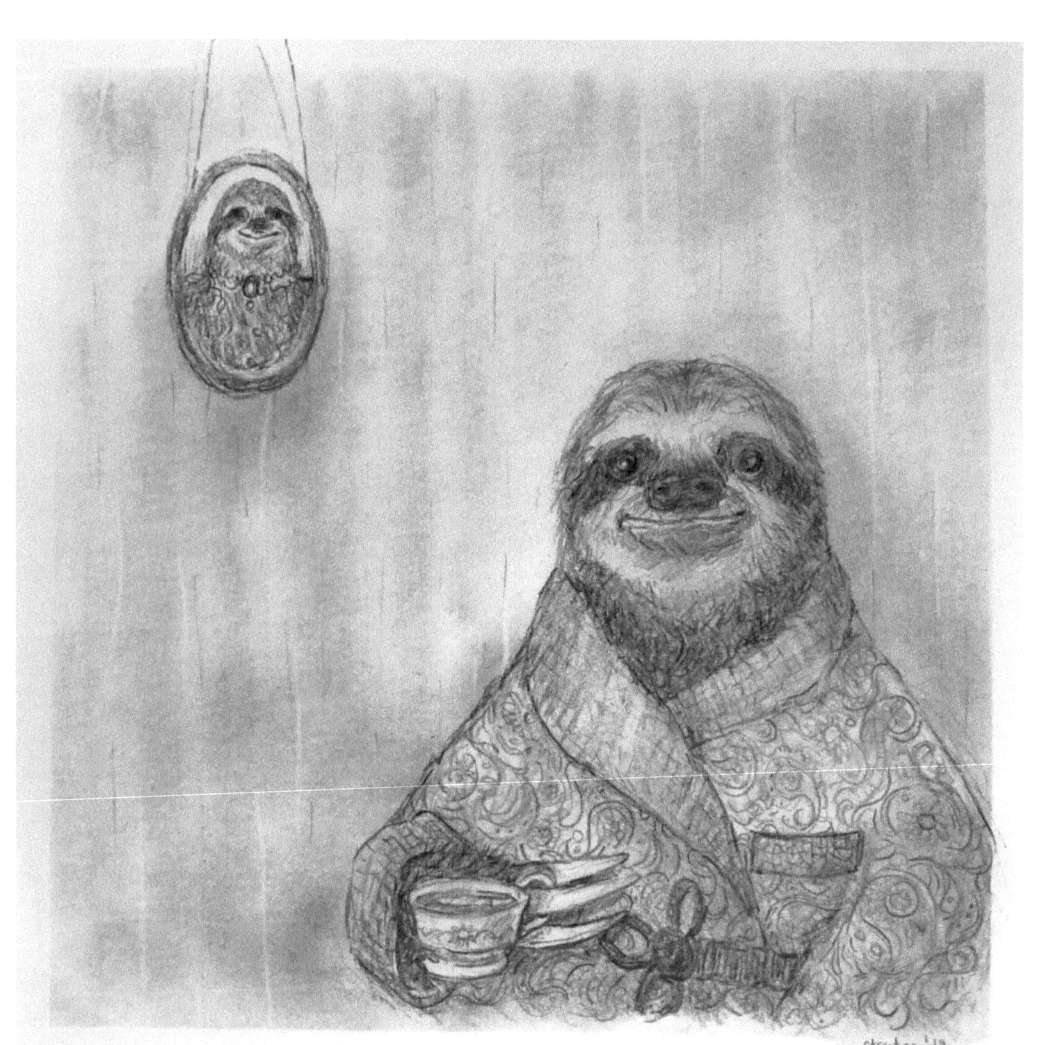

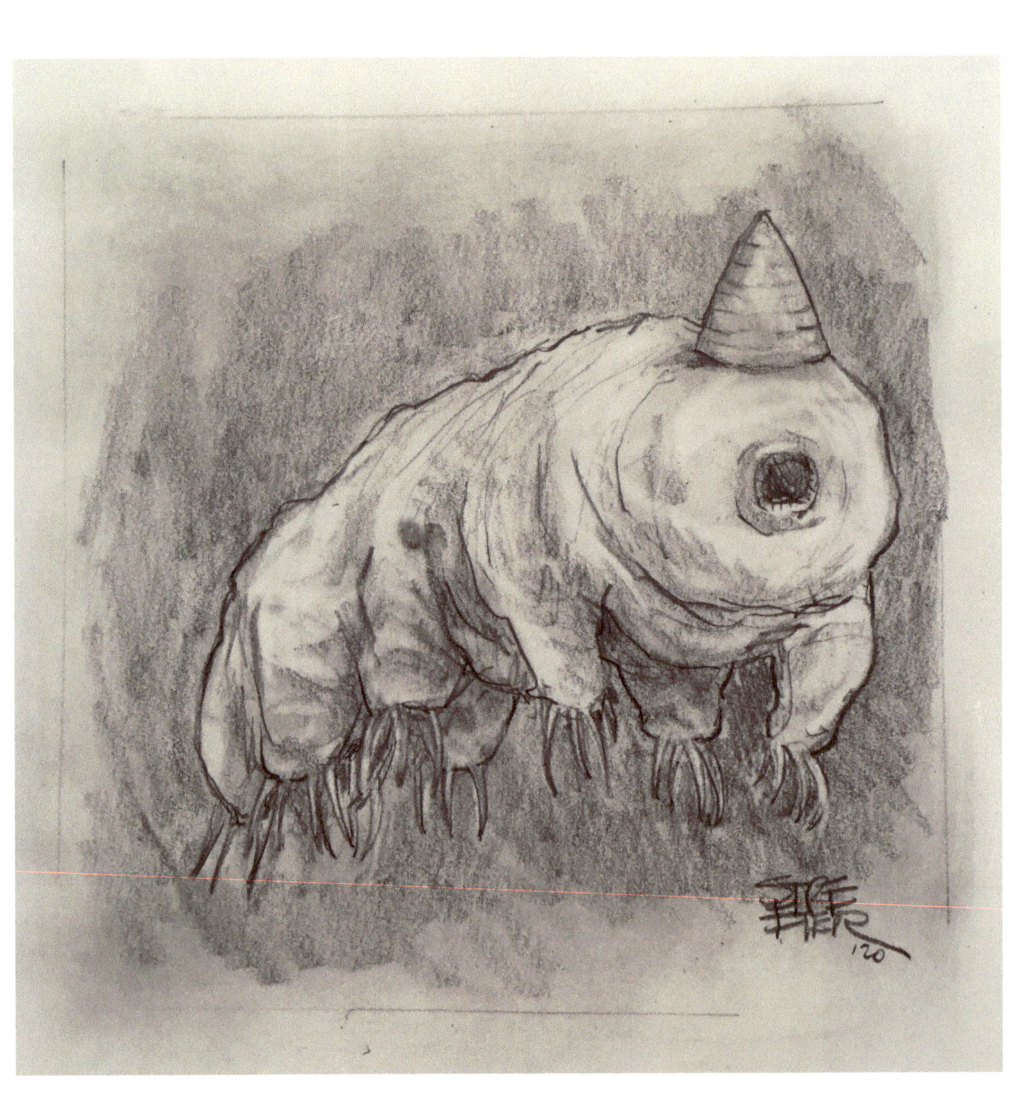

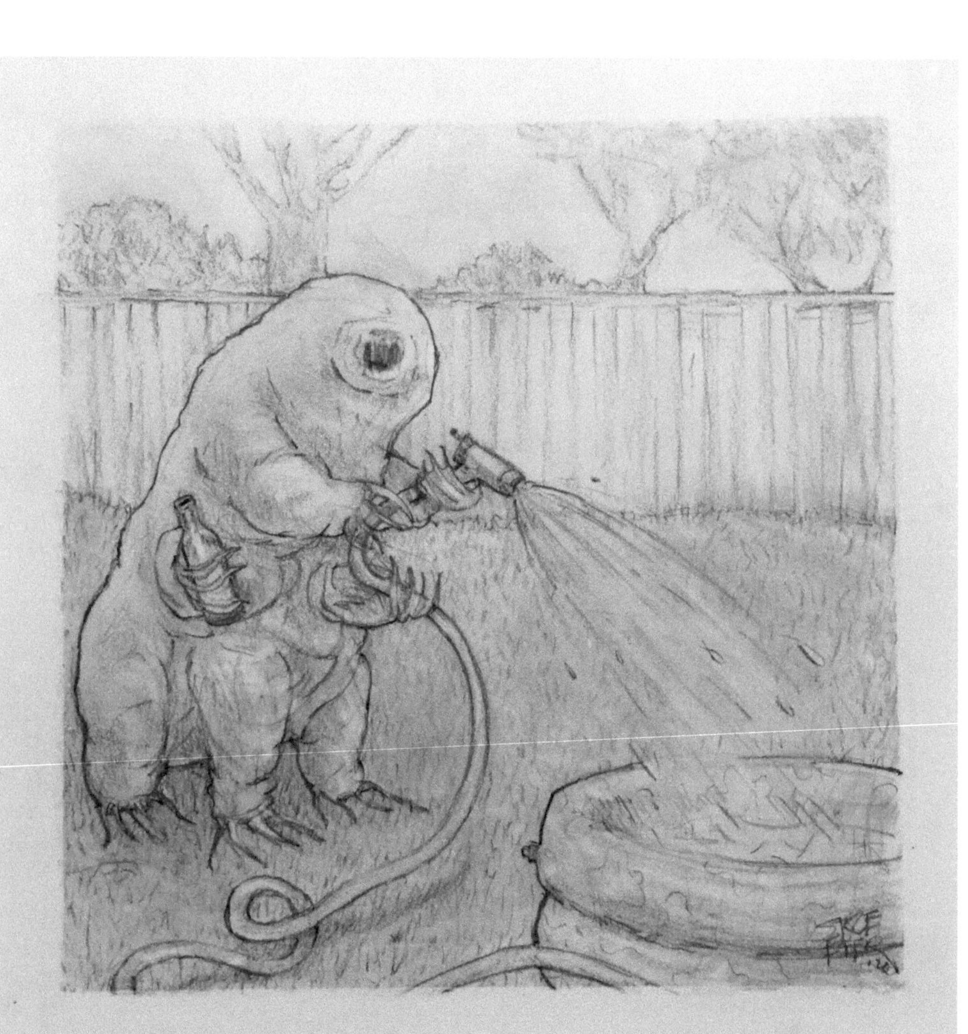

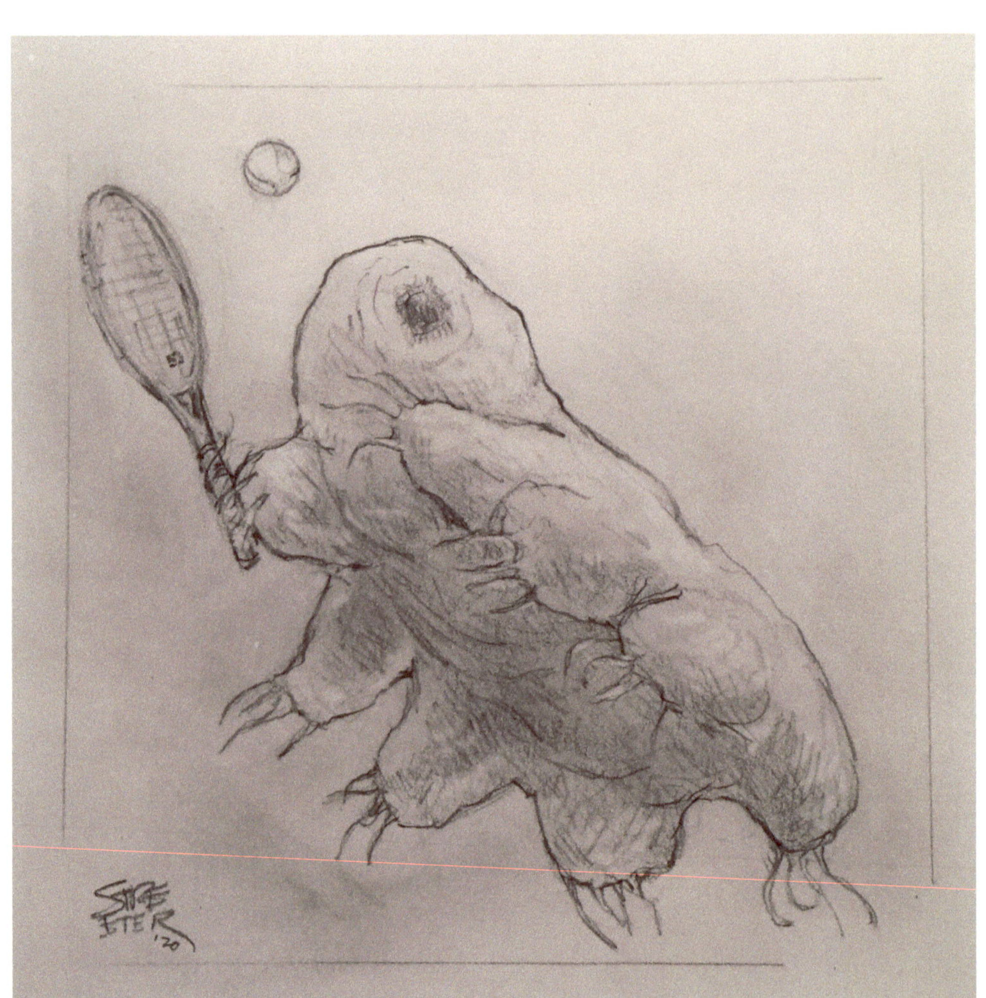

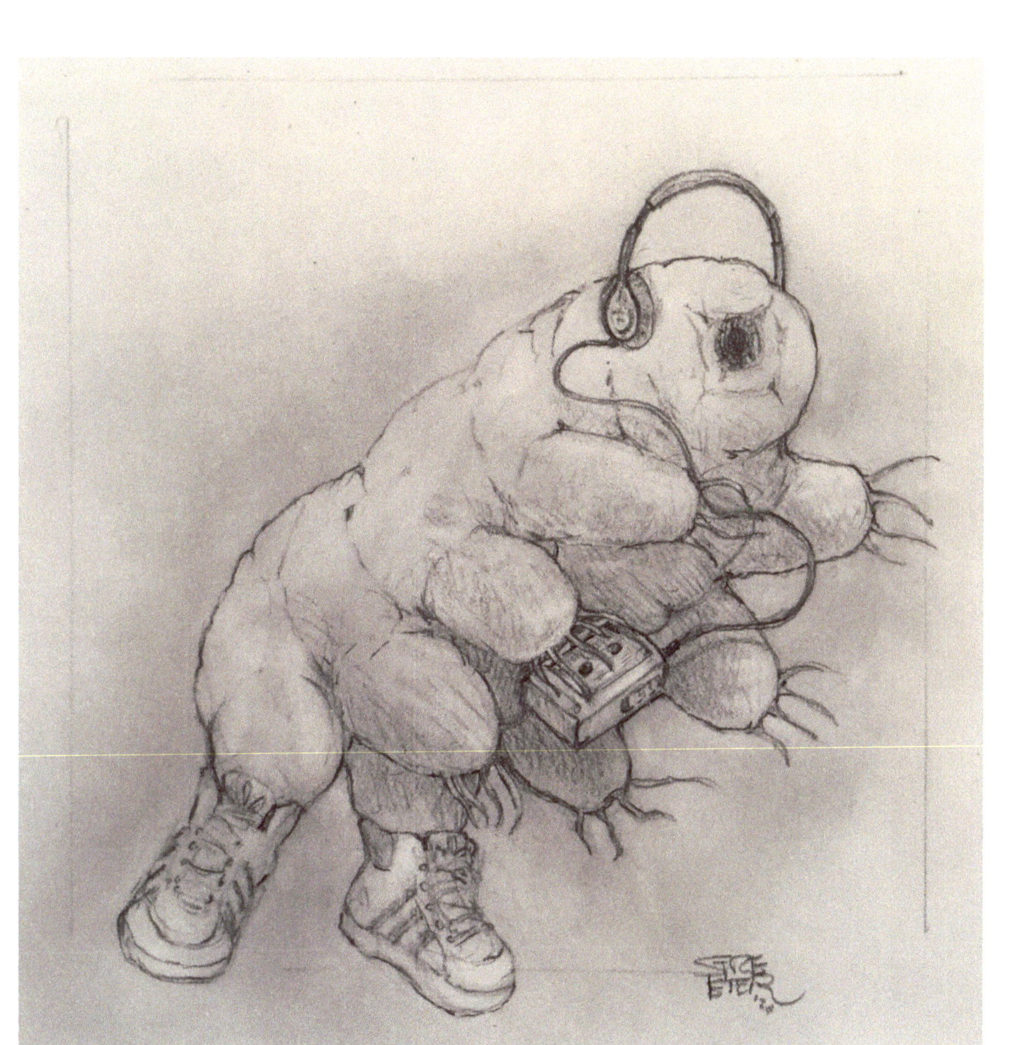

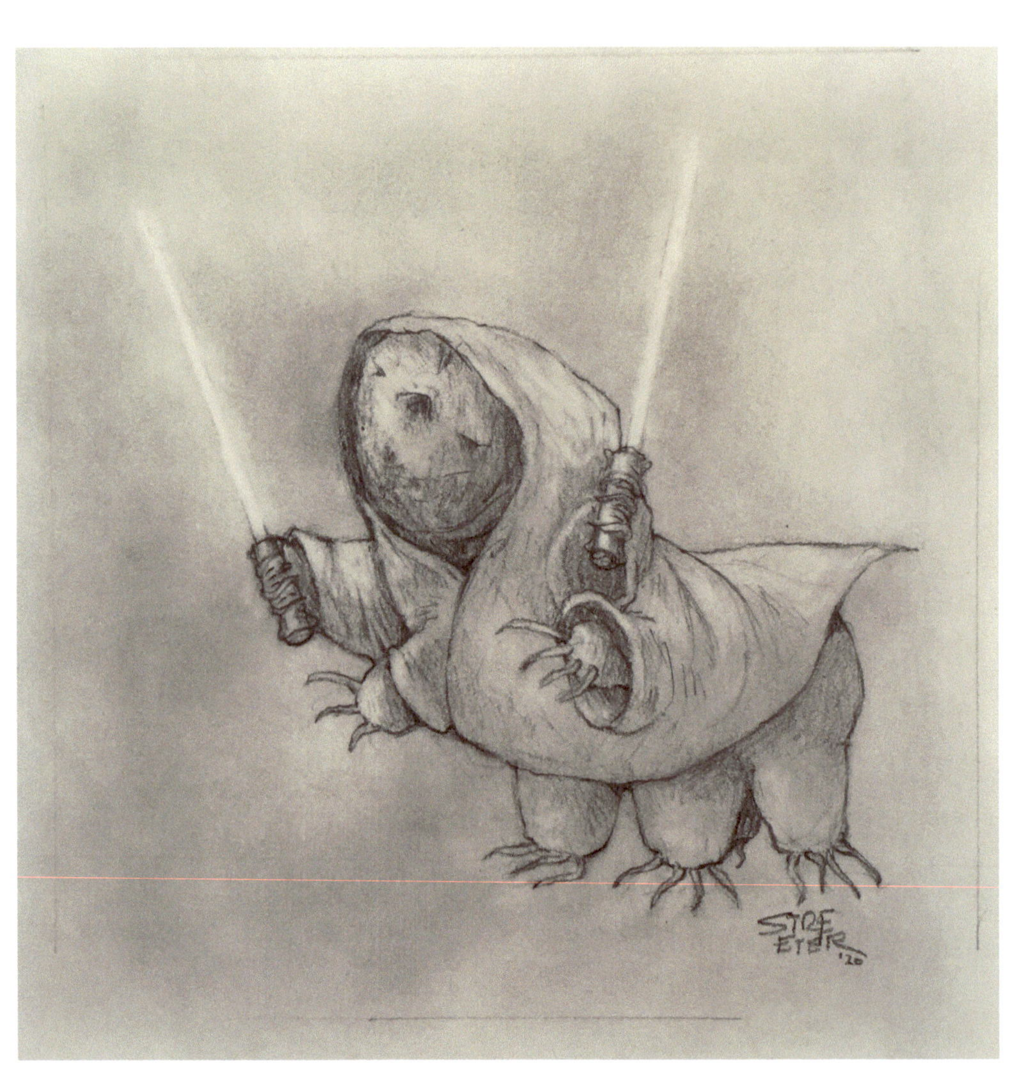

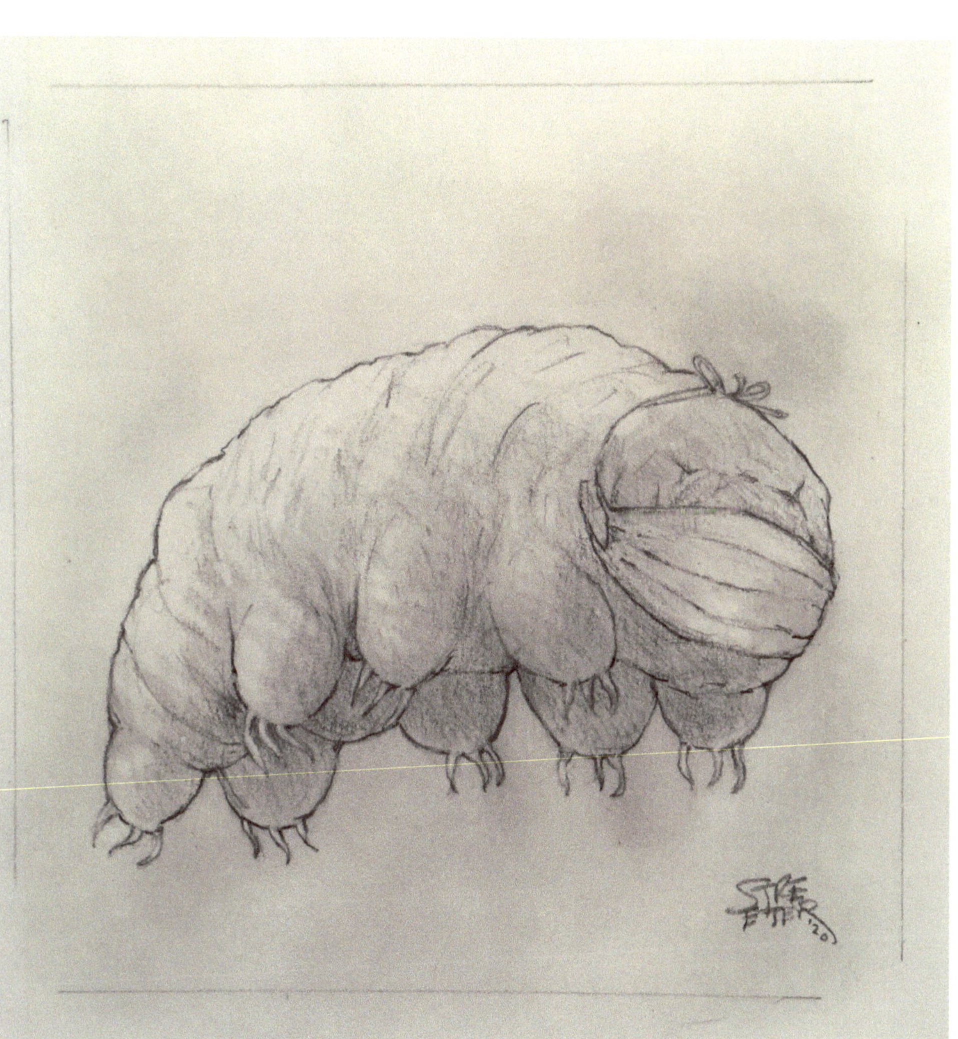

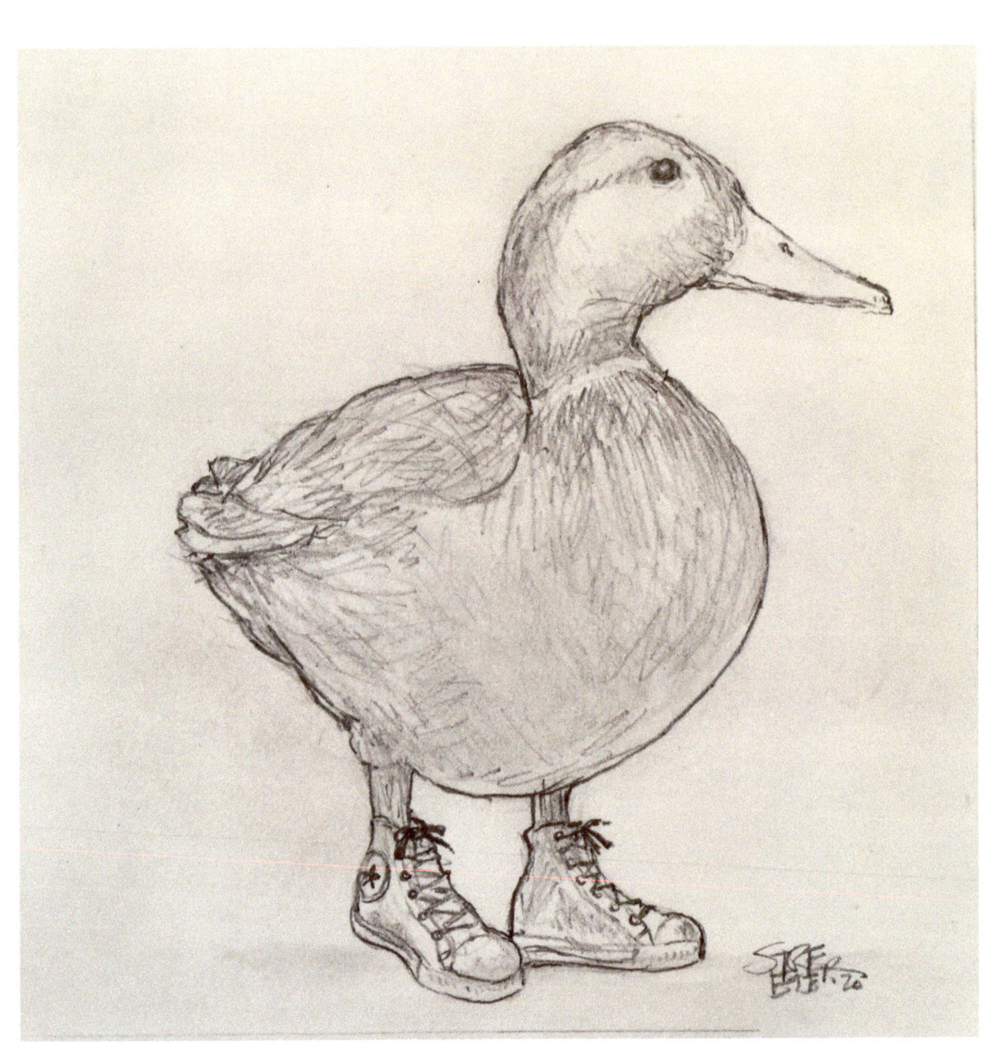

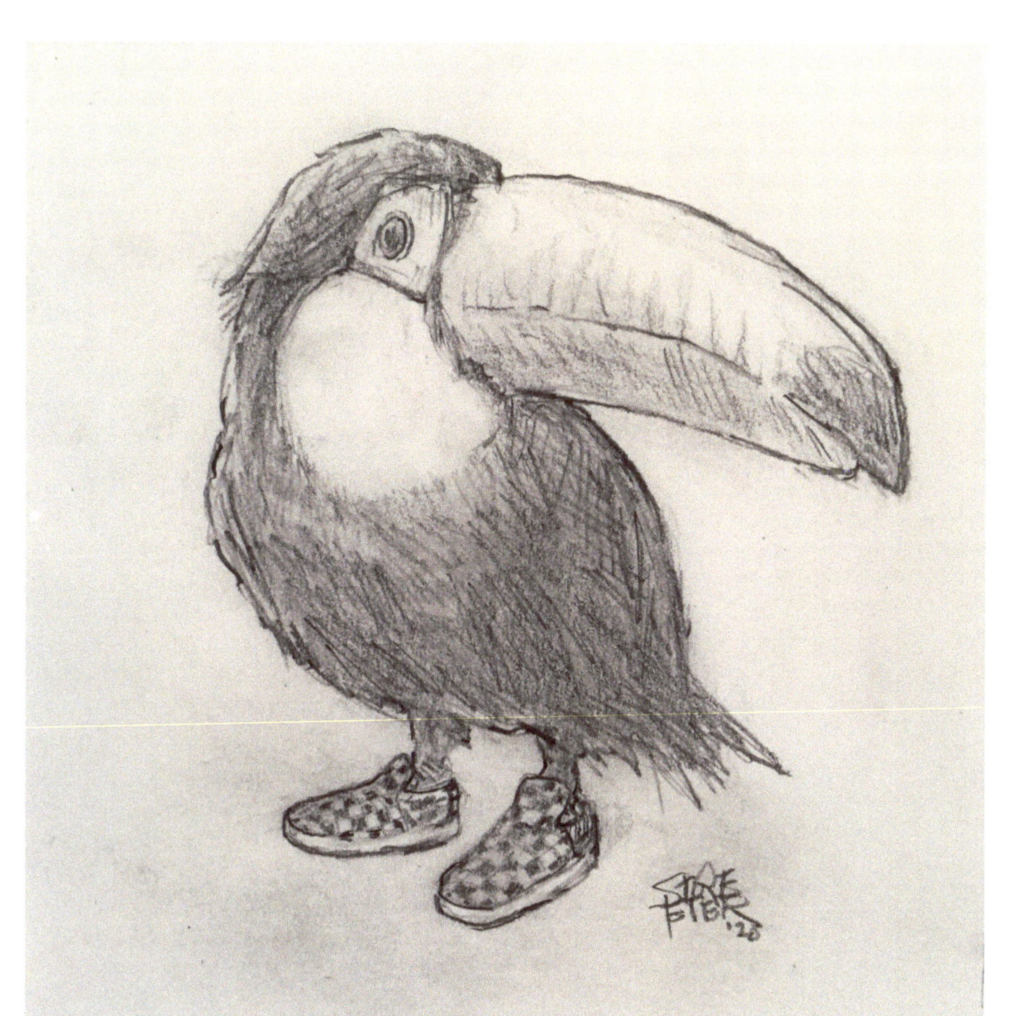

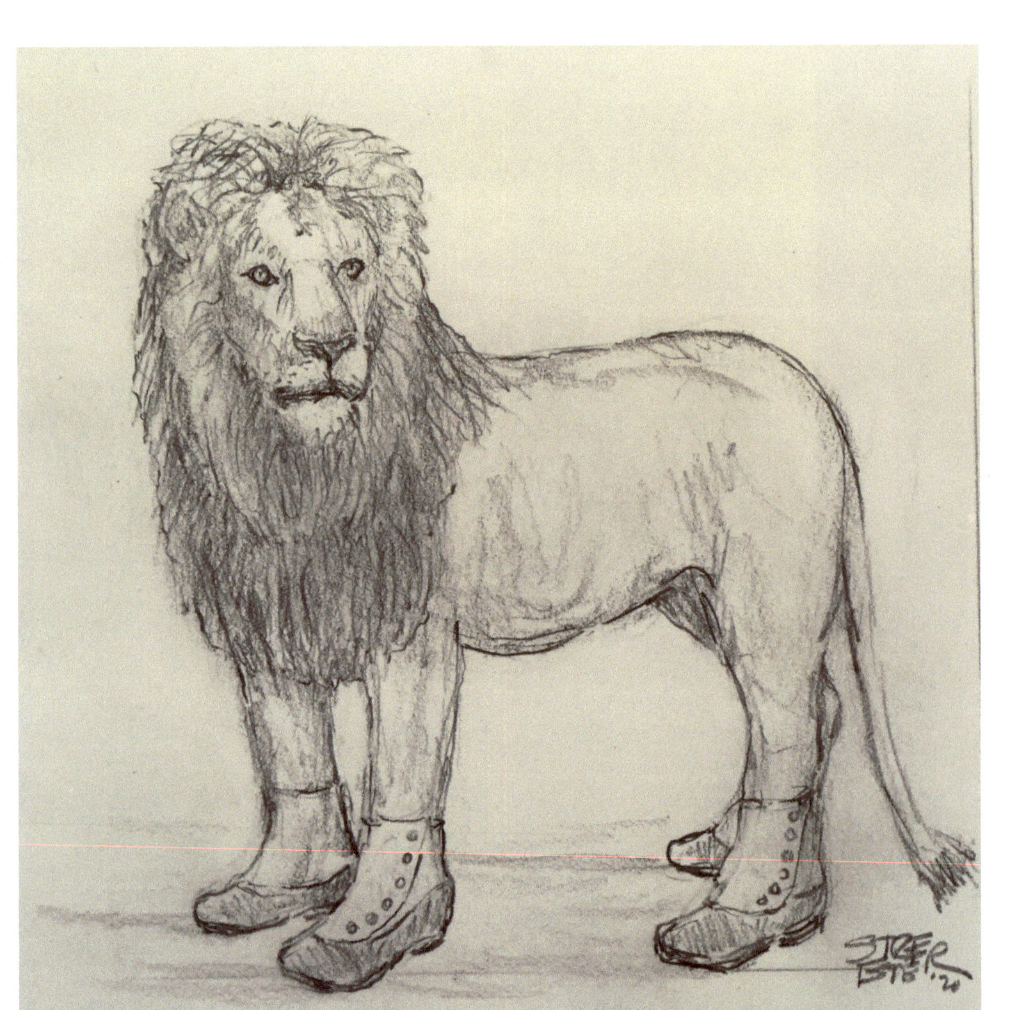

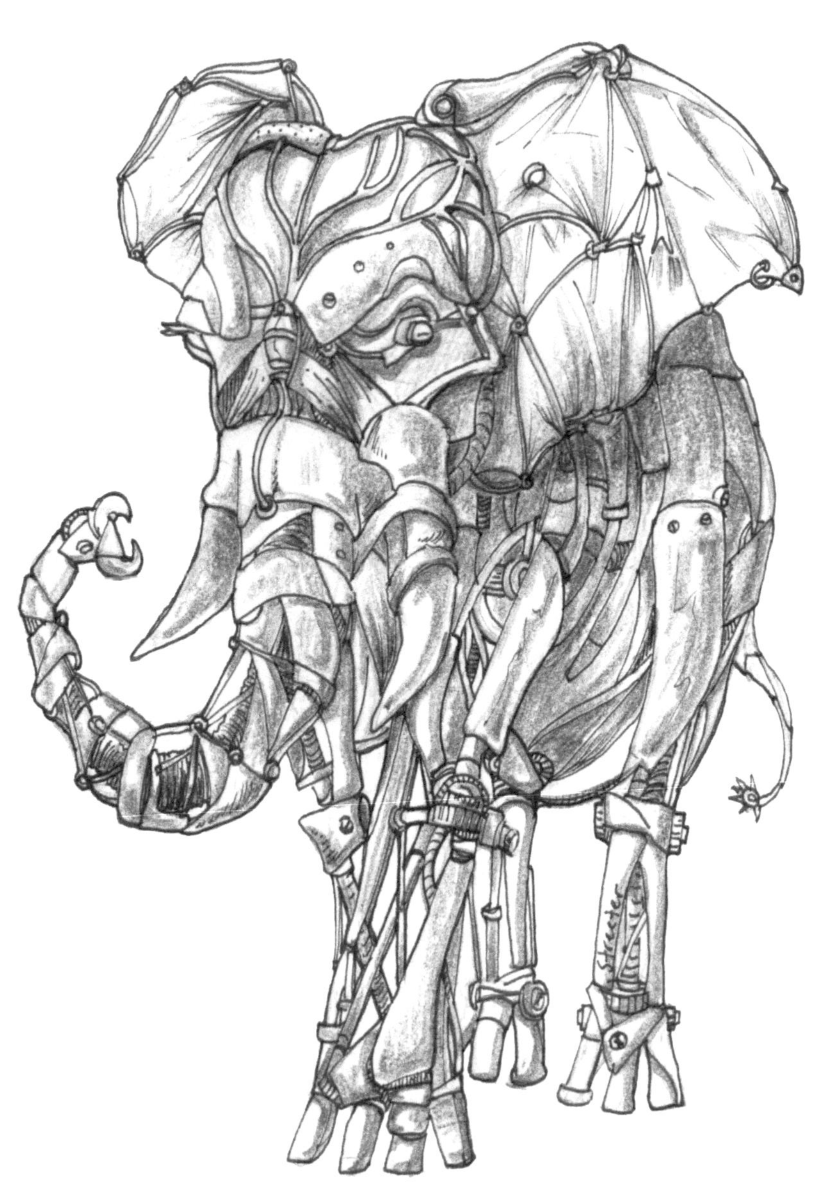

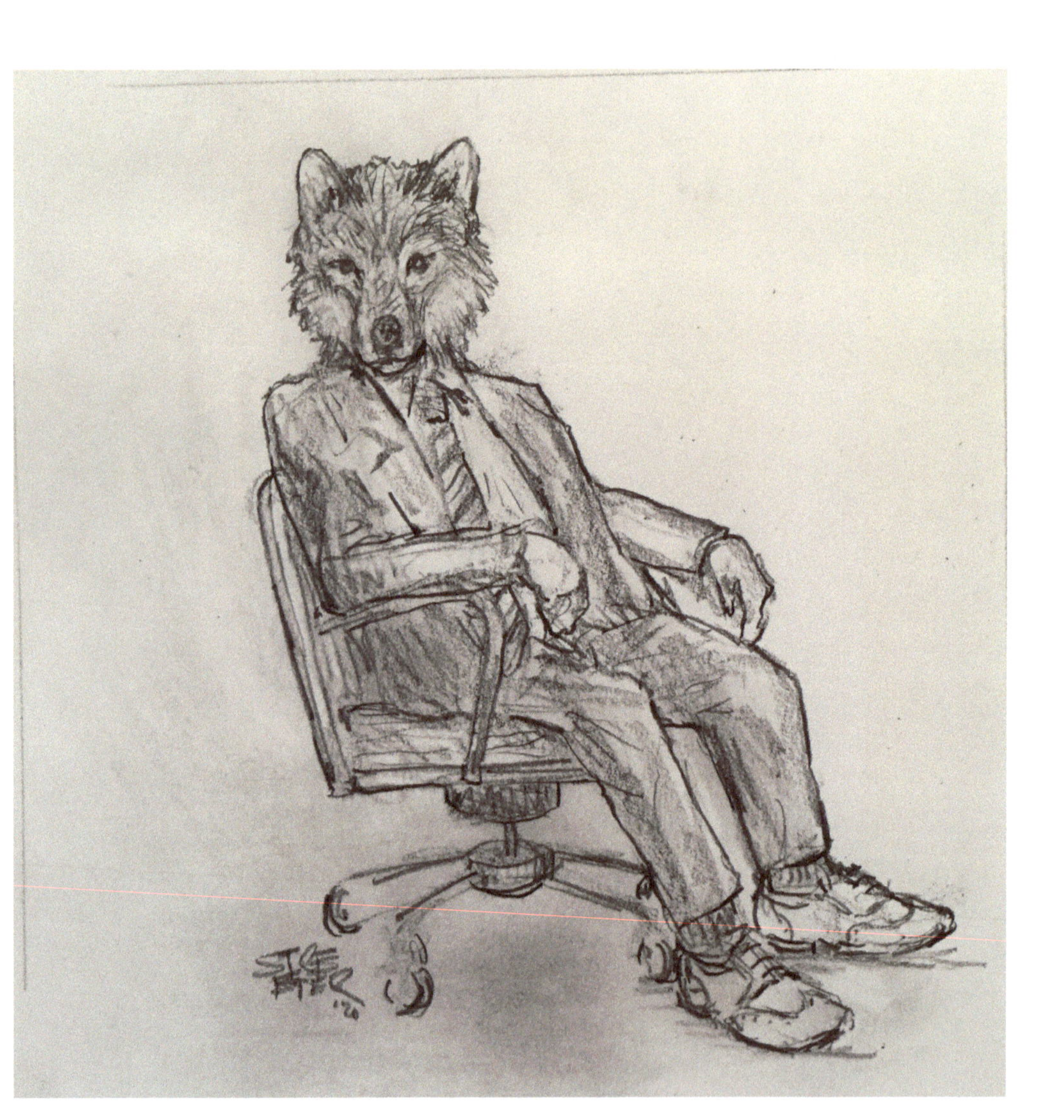

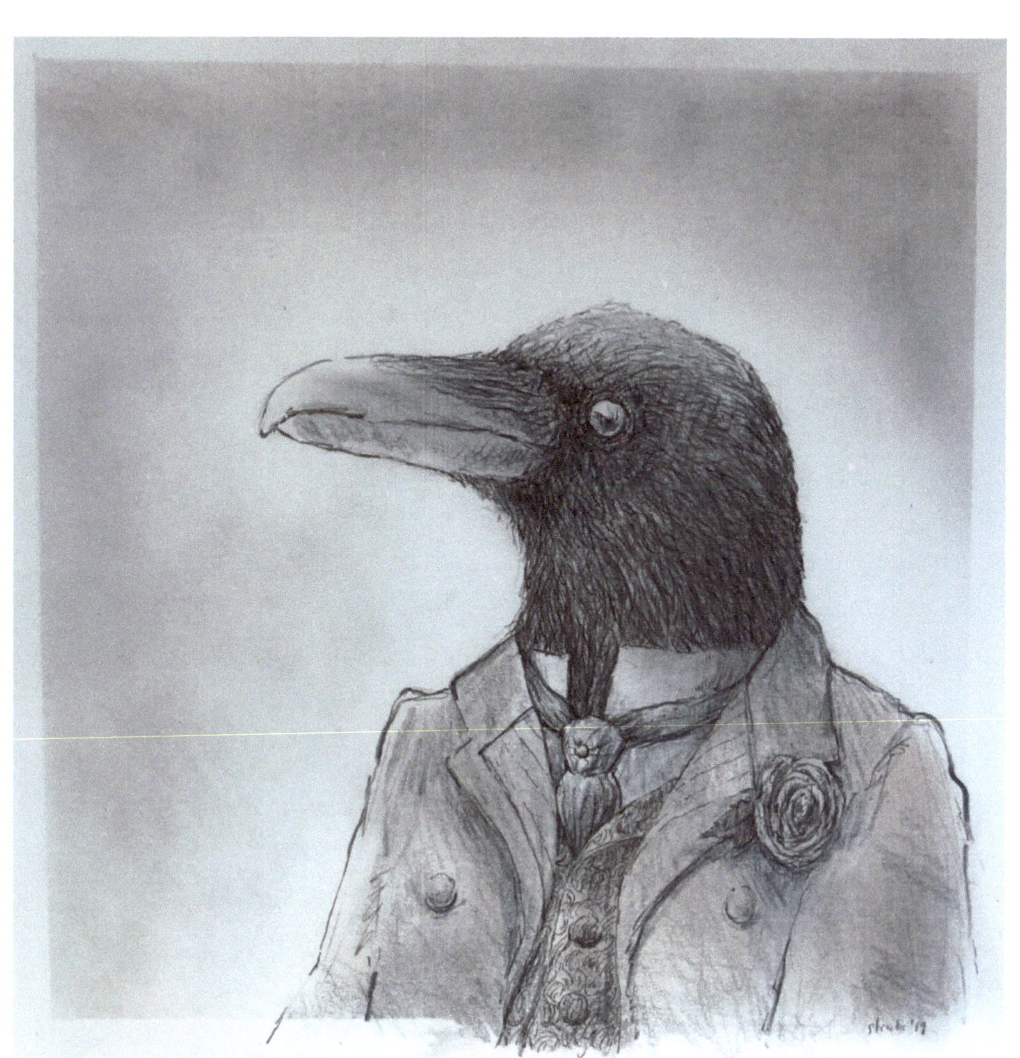

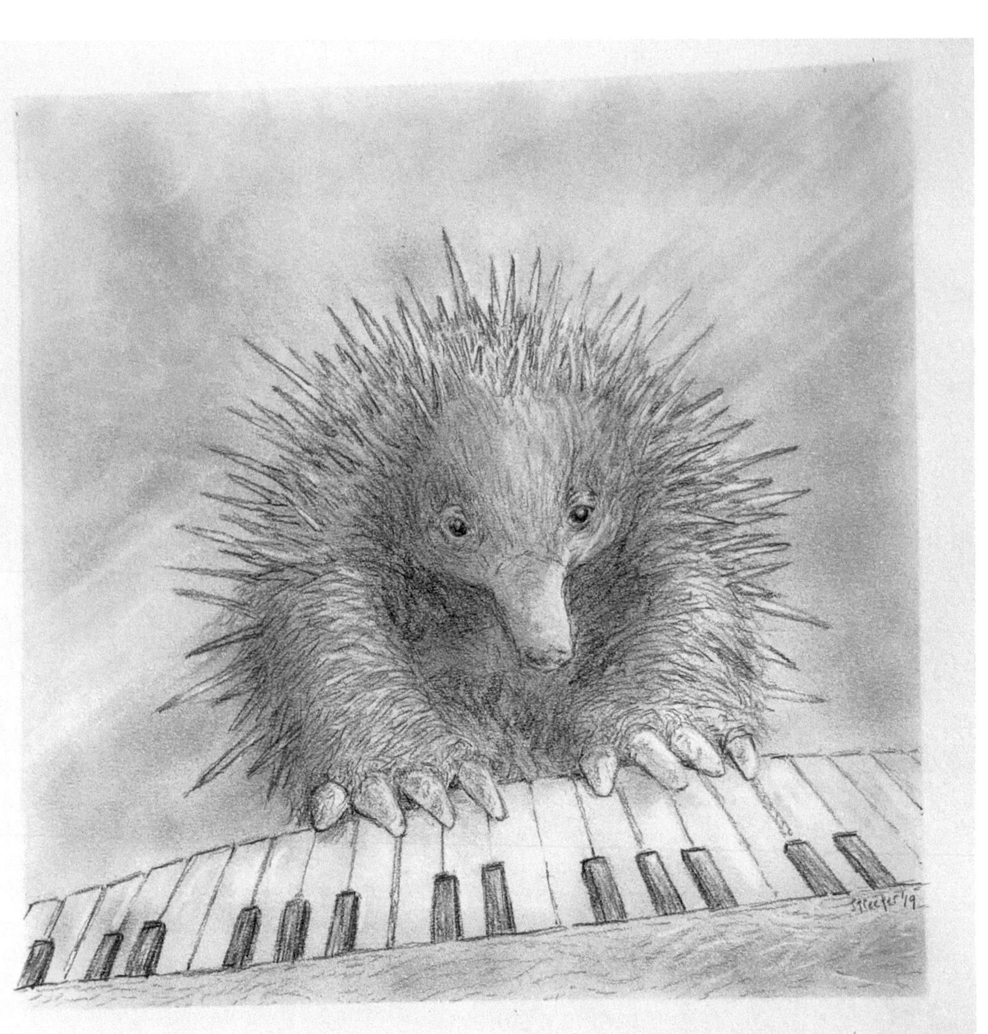

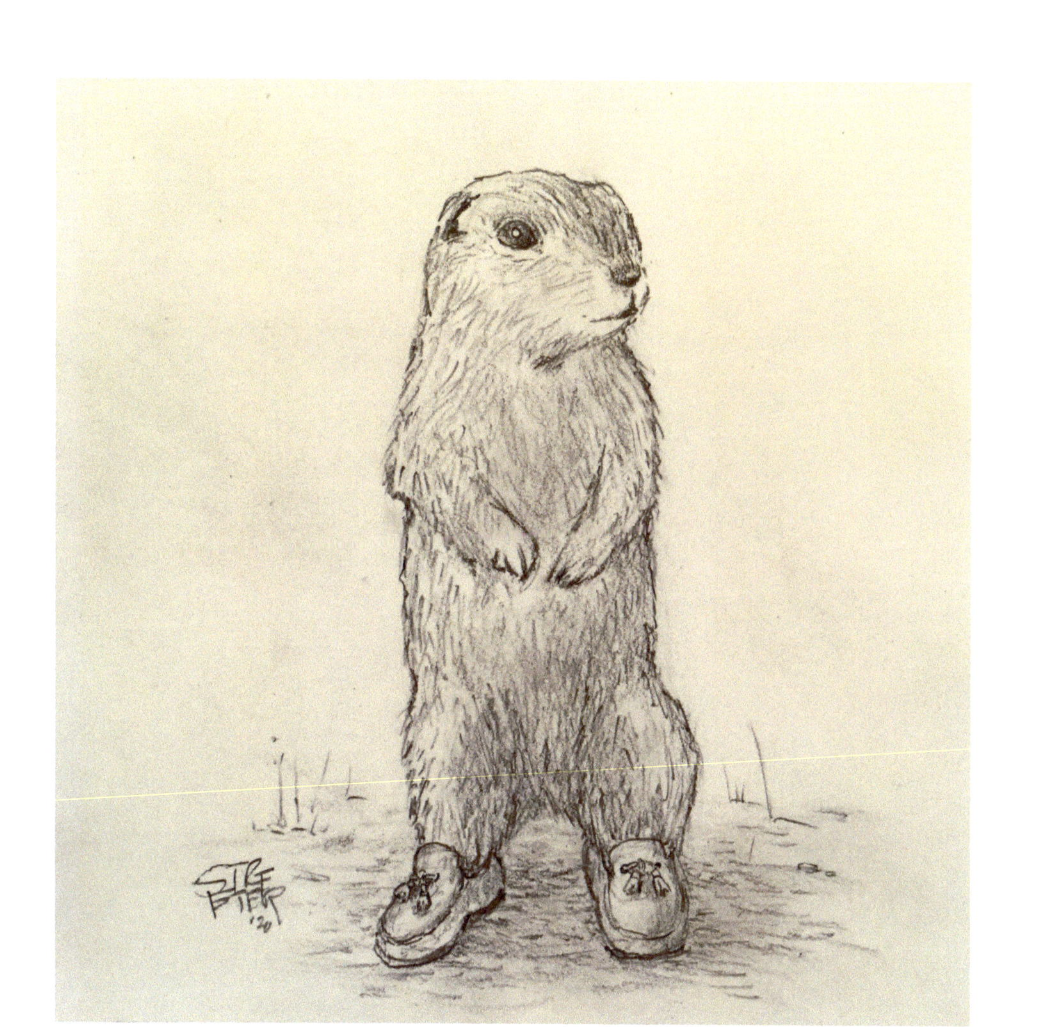

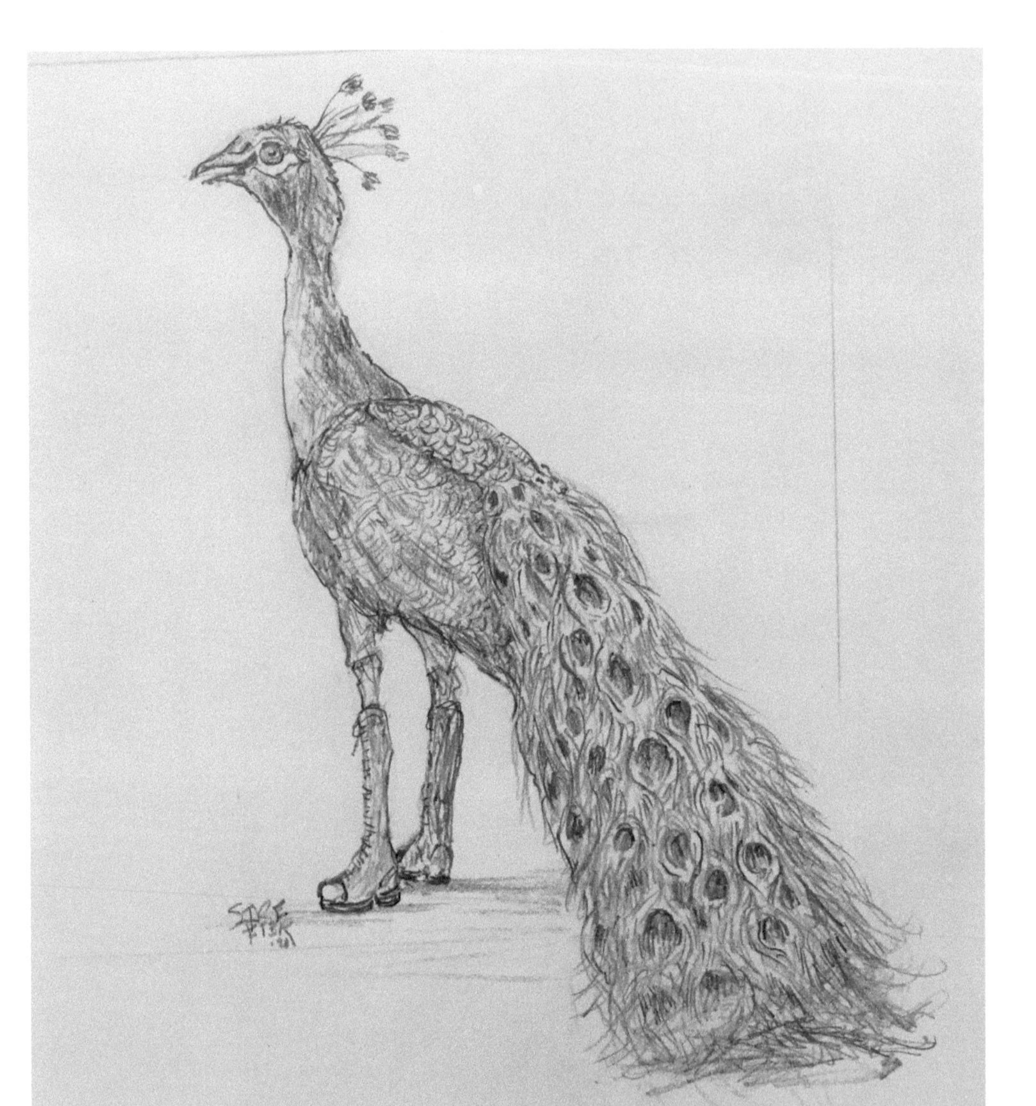

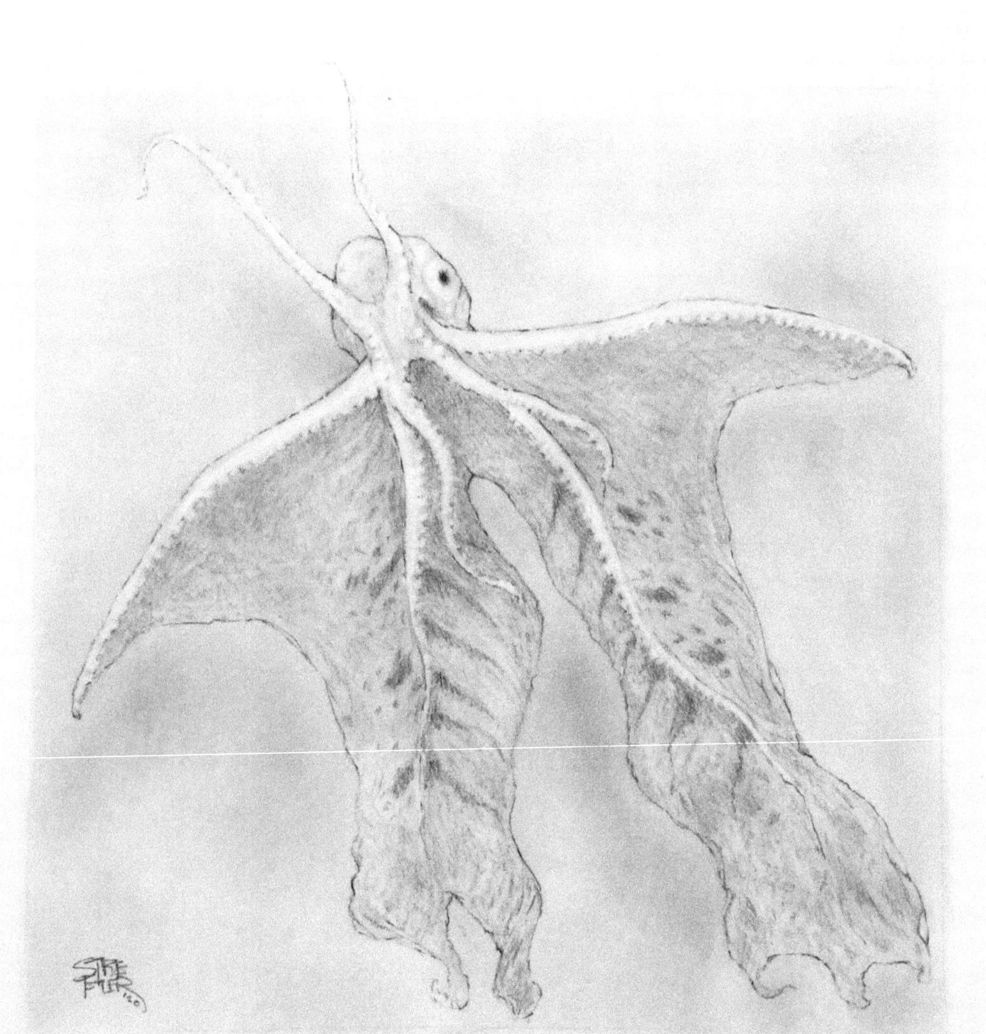

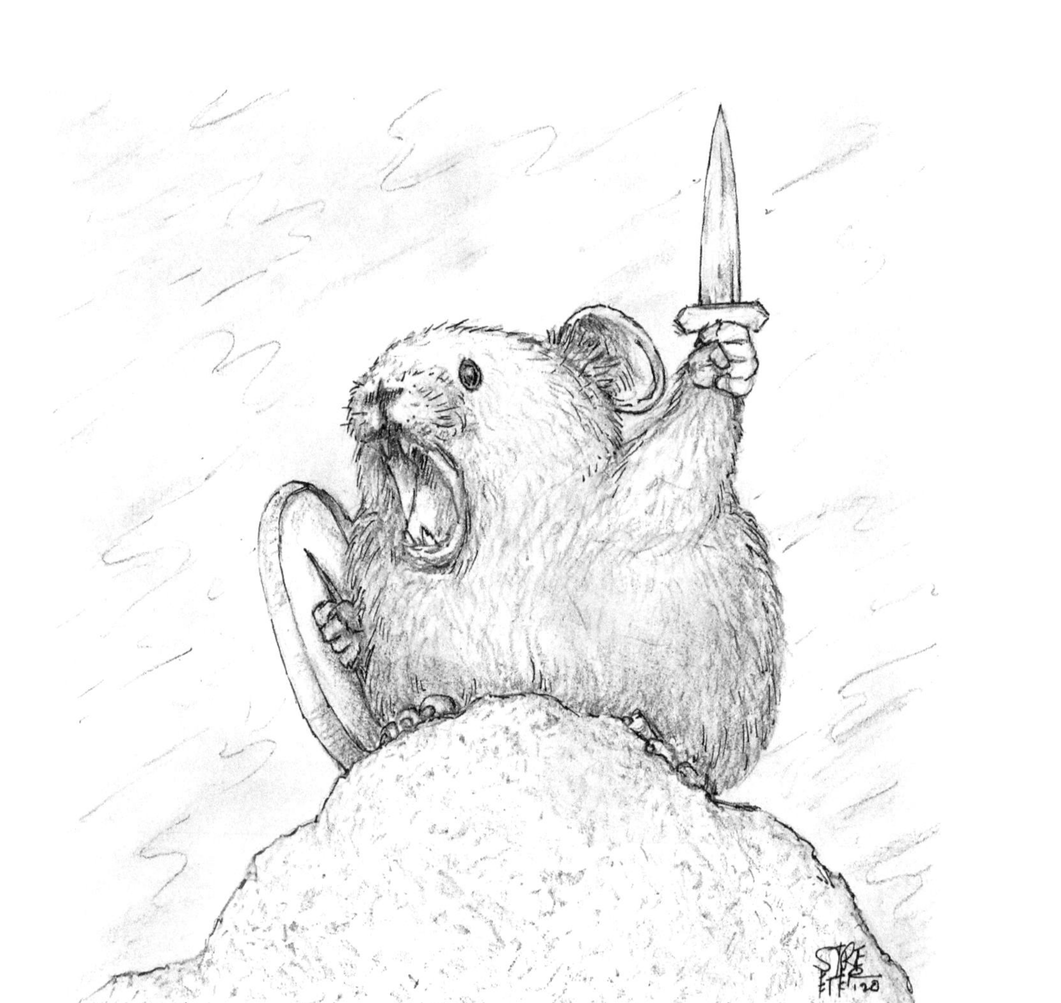

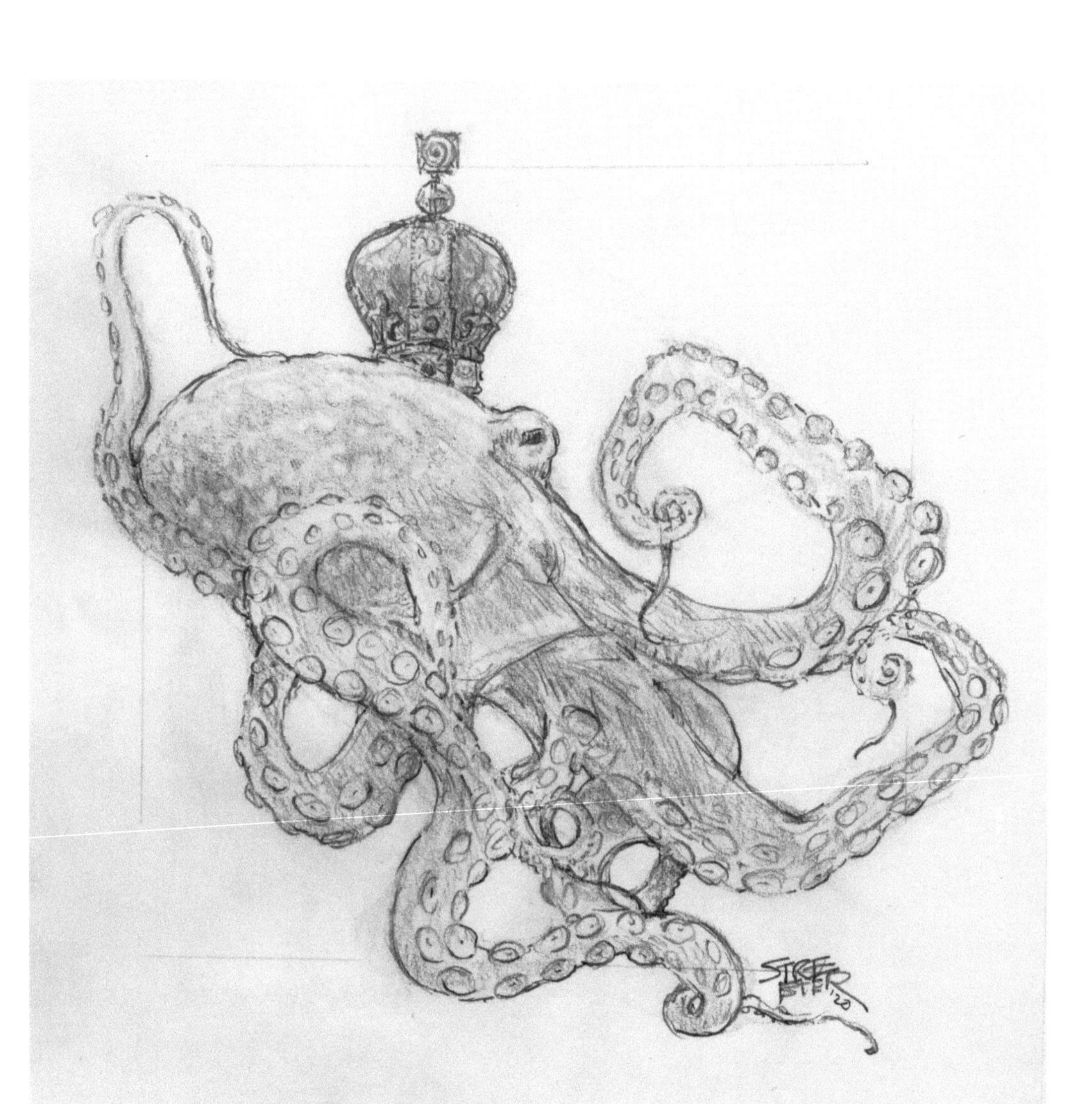

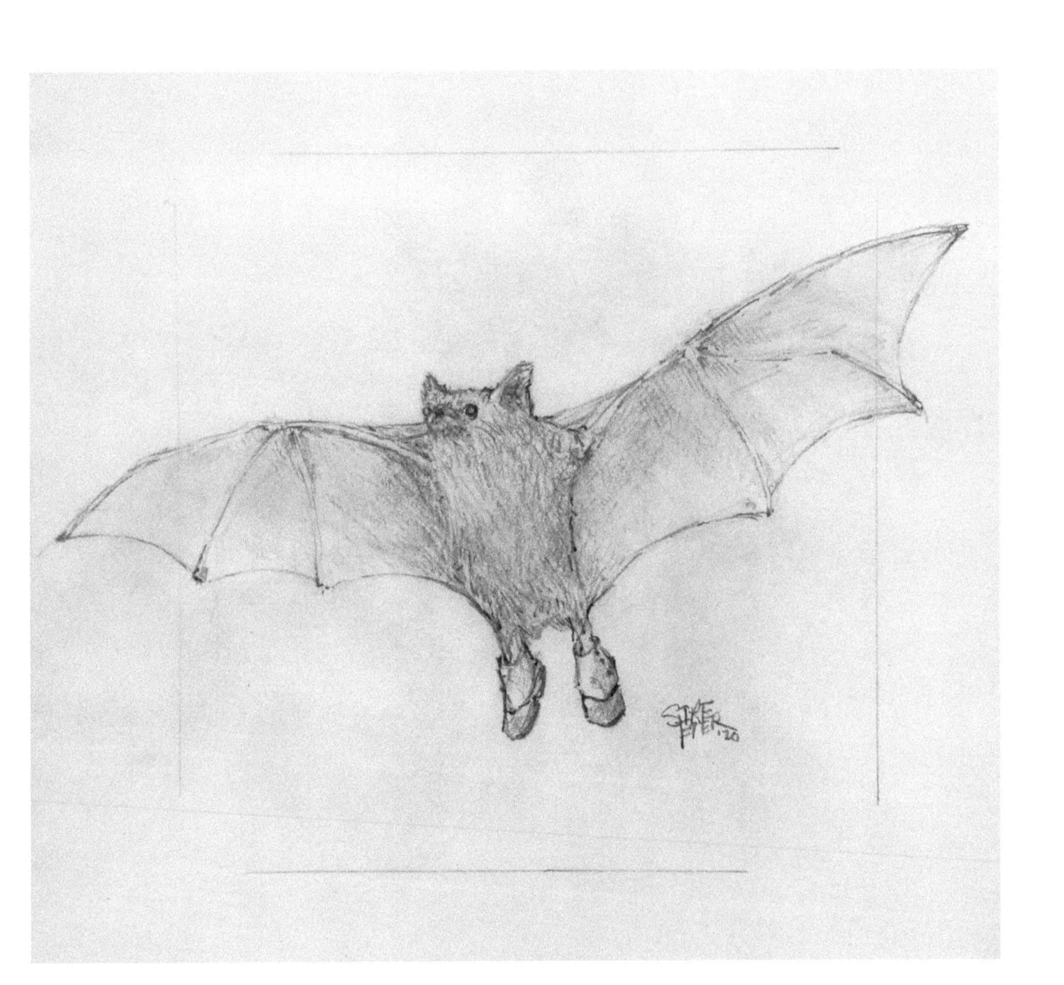

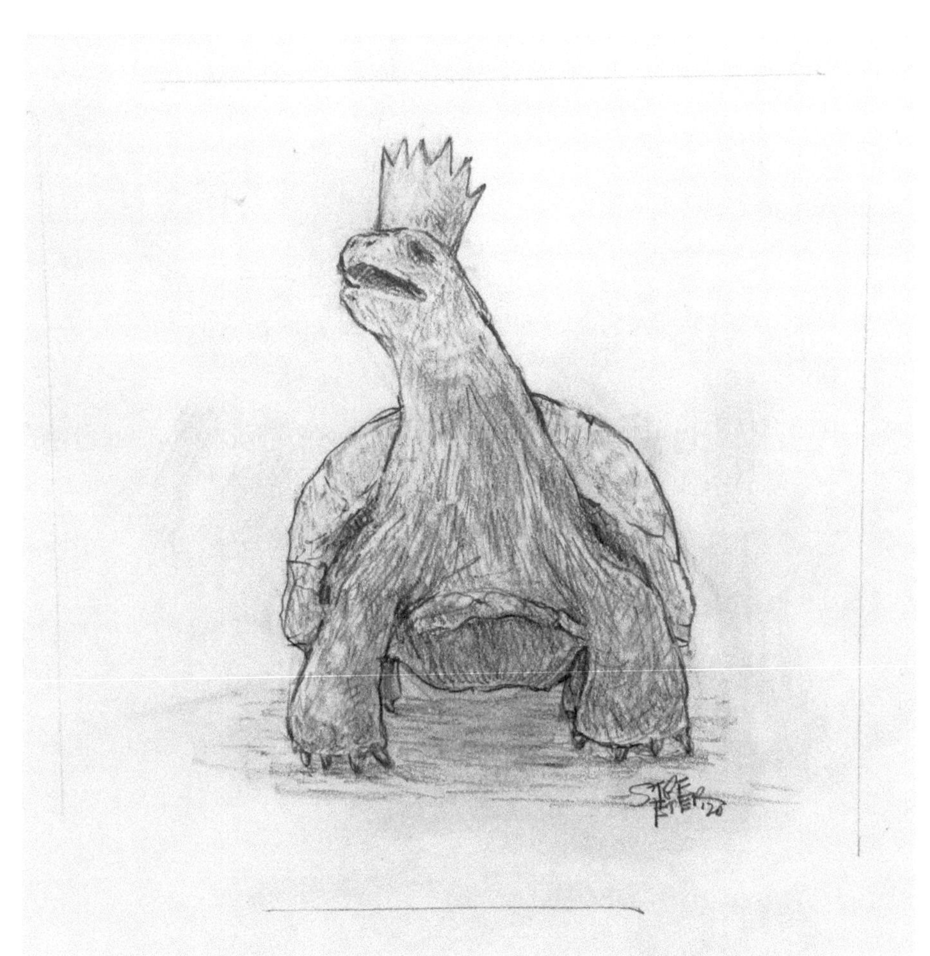

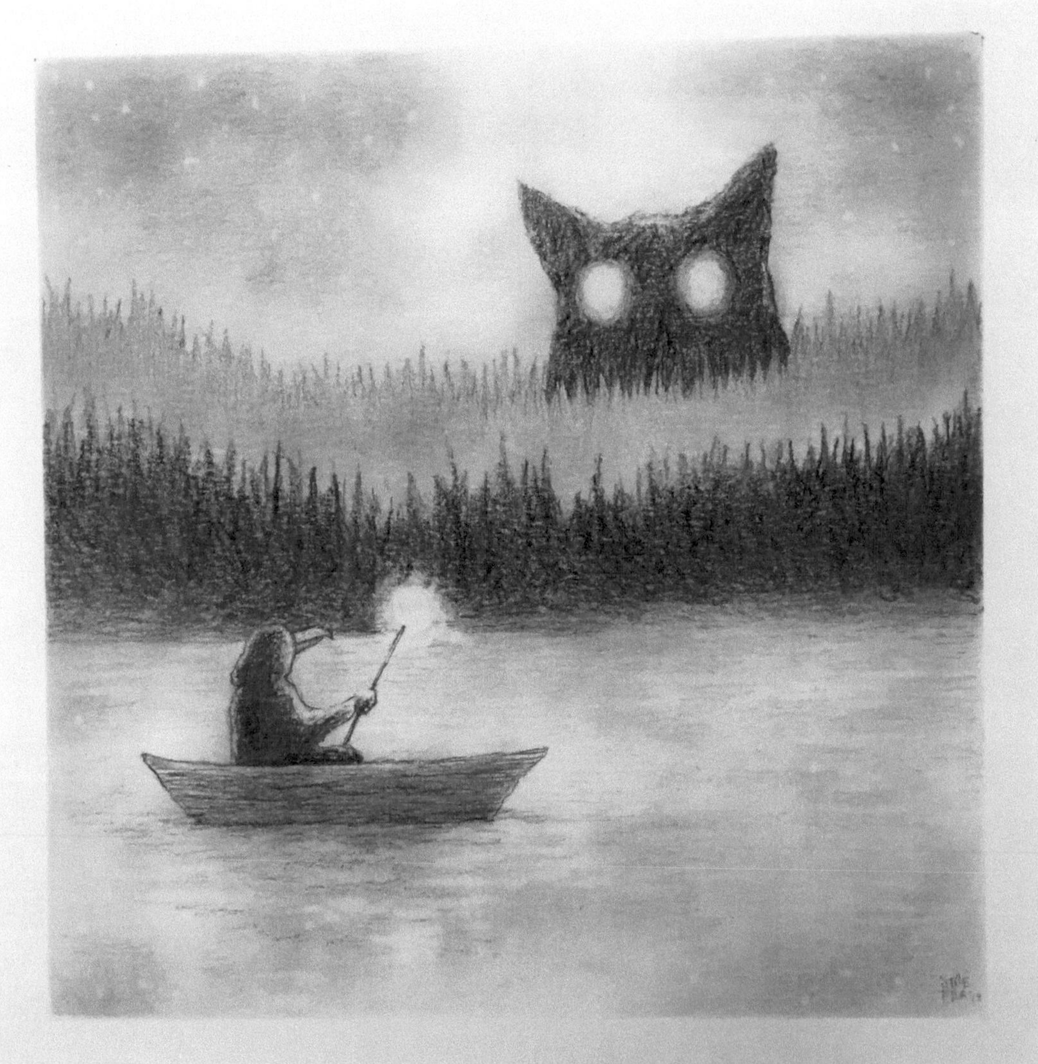

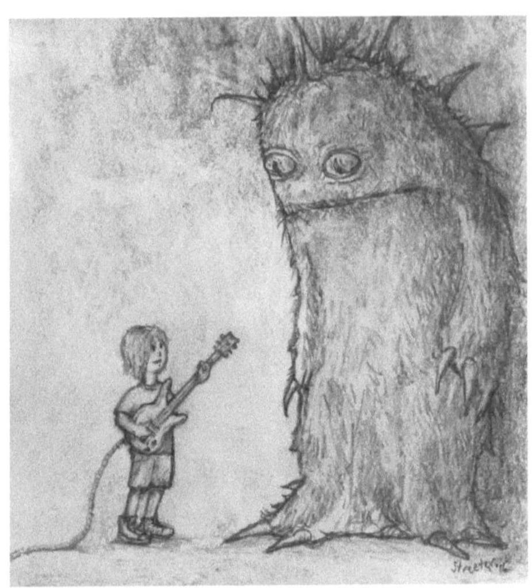

WATCH OUT FOR THE ARTIST

Betsy Streeter is a cartoonist and illustrator and the author of three novels and an illustrated science fiction serial. She is a Northern California (East Bay) native, and lives there with her family and a collection of art, books and music that do not fit in the allotted space.

One of her cartoons travels with the Smithsonian Astrophysics Observatory's exhibit on black holes, and if you look really closely, another of hers is taped to the cabinet in the office of Paul Giamatti's character in the movie, *San Andreas*. It's a joke about earthquake prediction... since you won't be able to read it. Or even see it. But it's there.